In the Shadow of "Excellence":

Recovering a Vision of Educational Opportunity for All

by Gregory J. Fritzberg

In the Shadow of "Excellence":
Recovering a Vision of Educational Opportunity for All

By Gregory J. Fritzberg

Published by Caddo Gap Press
3145 Geary Boulevard PMB 275
San Francisco, California 94118 U.S.A.
Alan H. Jones, Publisher

Cover Photograph of Aragaw Alemayehu
by Steve Ringman of *The Seattle Times*
Reproduced with Permission of *The Seattle Times*

ISBN 1-880192-30-6

Price $24.95 US

Library of Congress Cataloging-in-Publication Data

Fritzberg, Gregory J.
    In the shadow of "excellence" : recovering a vision of educational
opportunity for all / by Gregory J. Fritzberg.
        p.   cm.
    Includes bibliographical references (p.).
    ISBN 1-880192-30-6 (alk. paper)
    1. Educational equalization--United States. 2. Education and
state--United States.   I. Title.
LC213.2.F75   1999
379.2'6'0973--dc21   99-35901
                                                               CIP

Contents

Foreword

Equality of opportunity is an oft-invoked and much ignored ideal. Its neglect is partly the result of familiarity. Precisely because it is so integral to our self-image, we fail to consider it honestly and directly. But in addition, it is a difficult concept to understand. We can say that personal success should depend on individual talent and initiative, but we are not sure what such a proposition means, and we are even less sure what social arrangements would make it a reality. A serious examination of the subject requires a sophisticated grasp of political philosophy, sociology, and public policy—not a task for the intellectually faint of heart.

Gregory Fritzberg lacks neither the courage nor the ability for such a task. In this book he asks what it would take to achieve equal opportunity in the realm of education, and boldly crosses disciplinary boundaries to piece together the necessary elements of an answer. Along the way, he defends equality of opportunity as a worthy ideal, traces the uncertain history of government support for educational equality, identifies those children currently denied a decent chance to create successful lives, and articulates a set of far-reaching but eminently realizable reforms on behalf of educational opportunity for all citizens. He correctly insists that in a democratic society we cannot discuss education without discussing equal opportunity, and vice versa. Rightly conceived, education embodies the democratic values of freedom and equality: it gives all of us the tools needed for constructing our own lives.

By equality of opportunity, Fritzberg has in mind what he calls "authentic meritocracy," which stands for something rather different than prevailing usage has led us to believe. A genuine meritocracy requires a substantive and not merely formal conception of equal opportunity; it requires that citizens actually be given the resources to compete on a level playing field. And it requires, paradoxically, the elimination or at least delay of meritocratic classifications in primary and secondary schooling. Before citizens can compete on fair terms they must have received an equal educational endowment. One of the many surprises in this book is that meritocracy implies a much more robust commitment to equality than either its friends or critics have realized.

Fritzberg's account is sensitive to arguments from both the right and the left. His conclusions, though bold and even radical, are carefully drawn. This is an original and authoritative treatment of an important subject which no one interested in equality of opportunity, education, or democracy can afford to miss.

—Jamie Mayerfeld
Associate Professor of Political Science
University of Washington

Preface

In the introduction to *Liberal Equality* (1980), a book which has distinctively shaped my thinking concerning questions of distributive justice—i.e., Who gets what and why?—Amy Gutmann explains her interest in such questions in personal rather than academic terms. Simply put, Gutmann was raised and educated under comfortable economic circumstances and felt for those who were not so fortunate. Gutmann understands the utter arbitrariness of one's social origins, and *Liberal Equality* is an exploration of the different liberal political theories advanced over the years that have promoted more egalitarian societal arrangements. I share with Gutmann the enduring advantages of comfortable economic origins and plentiful educational opportunities, and I also share her awareness of those less advantaged. As a former youth minister and seminarian, I first articulated my concerns about social injustice in theological language. However, this book is an attempt to put my discomfort with inequality, and my more specific convictions about how the American educational system is implicated by it, in the more public language of liberal political theory.

Like Gutmann, I think that the liberal political philosophical paradigm possesses sufficient conceptual resources to help us envision a more just society, a society in which the life chances of children are not unduly influenced by ascriptive social background characteristics such as racial, social-class, or gender identity. The vision that guides this book concerns equality of opportunity, the idea that all children deserve an equal start in the "race" for educational, occupational, and economic rewards. I do not advocate strict equality of results—the attempt to eliminate the race completely by directly manipulating occupational positions and their attached rewards so that all social groups defined by race, class, or gender obtain equal prestige and wealth. This bears mentioning because I will refer to equality of results as a means of measuring the presence of equality of opportunity. But just that; while truly equalizing educational and occupational opportunities across social groups should lead to the narrowing of subsequent achievement differences between these groups, the moral emphasis is on the former and not the latter. Equity, or fairness, is the normative focus, not equality, or sameness, of outcomes.

The perceptive reader will see that my defense of what I call substantive, or authentic equality of educational and occupational opportunity is both radical and conservative at the same time. It is radical in that it recommends significant, ongoing transfers of wealth in order to fund expansive human capital development programs for the children of the poor so that they may develop their native talents in ways that give value to their formal political and economic liberties. As the primary public institution charged with nurturing our human capital, K-12 education requires much more support than it now receives. However, my argument for substantive equality of opportunity is conservative in that while it attempts to make our current economic race more procedurally fair, it does not challenge the way the race is defined in the first place. This book does not qualify as a post-modern critique of power relations and the Western industrial-capitalist regime. I do not wish to discount the importance of such an effort, but only to communicate that I do not attempt it here.

The contribution of this work to contemporary educational scholarship does not lie in what it says to educational stratification researchers, liberal political theorists, or students of educational policy, taken separately. Rather, the unique contribution of this work lies in the way that it draws together several different scholarly conversations in the service of two broad themes. First, we must recognize that the near universal respect for equality of opportunity can mask important differences in its definition and implementation. And second, we must create authentic equality of opportunity through reforming educational and other human capital-related services for disenfranchised, non-mainstream children. I do not envision academics as my sole audience, but seek to influence prospective and practicing teachers, school administrators, and policy-makers as well. In fact, in an applied academic field such as Educational Foundations—the field in which this book is intended to contribute—it would be disappointing if those outside the academy were not engaged.

Finally, this is a highly idealistic book. It attempts to conceptualize the role of K-12 education in what philosophers like to call the "good society." As I state in the conclusion, I am hopeful that my political vision might make people more sensitive to issues of distributive justice in education, but I am also aware that it is unlikely to alter the economic and political ethos of the day, especially given its statist implications and the high-profile failings of certain socialist regimes during recent years. In the beginning stages of my career, I wanted to articulate how I think things ought to be. I can spend the remainder of my career discovering why they are not that way.

◆ ◆ ◆ ◆ ◆

Dedications and Acknowledgements

I wish to dedicate this book to two special people: my wife Marie and my young friend, Aragaw Alemayehu. Marie graciously supported me throughout the research and writing process. She supported me financially during the first years of the doctoral studies that led to this project. She supported me domestically from beginning to end, providing leadership in our home and caring for two children who were not yet born when I typed the first sentence, Emma Jane and Ethan James. Finally, she supported me professionally, serving as a loyal but candid critic of my ideas and their expression. It is not merely good manners to acknowledge that the work could not have been completed without her, and I am deeply grateful.

Aragaw, whose photograph graces the front cover, possesses that mysterious quality that we call resilience, a quality which has enabled him to march spirit-intact through a less-than-perfect educational experience in the Seattle Public Schools upon his arrival at the age of nine from Sudan. Aragaw's enduring hope and winsome character have been a source of great joy for me, and I feel fortunate that our lives have overlapped.

I wish to publicly thank Deborah Kerdeman, Michael Knapp, and Kenneth Sirotnik at the University of Washington for their caring and careful attention to the project from its formulation to its completion. I wish to thank Scott Miller at the College Board in New York and Steven Tozer at the University of Illinois at Chicago for reviewing the book in its final form and gracefully encouraging me at the same time they offered suggestions for future research. Sharon Westre provided very helpful editorial assistance at this stage, proof-reading the manuscript and teaching me some new things about writing in the process. I also wish to thank Alan Jones at Caddo Gap Press in San Francisco for bringing the work to publication, and especially for his responsiveness and professionalism throughout the process. Finally, I wish to express heartfelt appreciation to Jamie Mayerfeld at the University of Washington for taking time to initiate me into the world of political theory, and for being both kind and insightful as I sought to apply some new theoretical lenses to the realm of pre-collegiate education.

—Gregory Fritzberg
Spokane, Washington

Most social systems need a lightning conductor. The formula which supplies it to our own is equality of opportunity. The conception is one to which homage is paid today by all, including those who resist most strenuously attempts to apply it. But the rhetorical tribute which it receives appears sometimes to be paid on the understanding that it shall be content with ceremonial honours. It retains its throne, on condition that it refrains from meddling with the profitable business of the factory and market-place. Its credit is good, as long as it does not venture to cash its cheques. Like other respectable principles, it is encouraged to reign, provided that it does not attempt to rule.

—R. H. Tawney, 1929

Chapter One

Introduction:
The Recent Neglect of Equality of Opportunity in American Educational Policy

I. The Recent Preoccupation with Educational "Excellence"

Goals 2000 and the Clinton Educational Agenda

In March of 1994, President Bill Clinton signed into law the *Goals 2000: Educate America Act*, which outlines comprehensively his administration's strategy for education reform. In some respects, *Goals 2000* represents a significant departure from *America 2000*, the previous Republican educational agenda. For example, Clinton replaces the Republican penchant for state and local decentralization with what Peter Cookson, Jr. calls a "new federalism" (1995, p. 406). He offers a systemic reform plan in which the federal government plays the leading role in designing curriculum frameworks, performance standards, and assessment strategies, although state adoption of these policies is strictly voluntary. Also, while Clinton favors proposals that introduce elements of choice and competition into public school systems, his faith in government as a force for good leads him to reject private school choice as a viable reform strategy.

At the same time, however, Clinton's remarks upon signing *Goals 2000* demonstrate that his perception of the primary purposes of schooling is quite similar to that of his predecessors. Speaking to a multiethnic student body gathered around a basketball court at award-winning Zamorano Fine Arts Academy in San Diego, California, Clinton observed: "You look like America will look in the 21st century, and we will have to win with you... [*Goals 2000*] sets world-class education standards for what every child at every American school should know in order to win when he or she becomes an adult" (Cummings, 1994, p. 5). Most likely, Clinton's curious emphasis on "winning" was rhetorically connected to the basketball court on which he was speaking, but this emphasis is still instructive.

In speaking of winning, Clinton echoes a concern for international economic competitiveness that has dominated American educational policy-making for the last decade and a half. Throughout this time, business and government leaders have been concerned with what they perceive to be a slippage in the United States' economic standing relative to Western Europe and Japan. The recent decline in global economic standing is considered by many to be a manifestation of human capital deficiencies.[1] Human capital deficiencies, so the argument goes, are themselves manifestations of educational failures, since schools are the primary institution responsible for providing academic and vocational skills, or capital, to the American population. Clinton joins his Republican predecessors in identifying economic competitiveness as a primary national goal and approaching educational policy-making from this perspective. His subordinates in the Department of Education, upon the introduction of *Goals 2000*, characterized it as the centerpiece of Clinton's "human capital agenda" for the nation (Smith & Scoll, 1995, p. 389).

The Crisis Rhetoric
Behind Current Education Reform

The popular belief that an educational crisis lay beneath America's economic struggles took hold in the early 1980s with the appearance of several reports on schooling commissioned by both private and public sources (see, for example, *A Nation at Risk*, 1983; *Action for Excellence*, 1983; *Making the Grade*, 1983). These reports described in sensational terms the academic under-performance of contemporary American students in relation to their international peers and to previous American generations. Consider, for example, the often-quoted opening paragraph of *A Nation at Risk*:

> Our Nation is at risk. Our once unchallenged preeminence in commerce, industry, science, and technological innovation is being overtaken by competitors throughout the world... the educational foundations of our society are presently being eroded by a rising tide of mediocrity that threatens our very future as a Nation and a people (National Commission on Excellence in Education, 1983, p. 113).

The empirical integrity of most of these reports has been challenged by reviewers since their publication. Following Lawrence C. Stedman and Marshall S. Smith (1983), Paul E. Peterson (1985), Gerald W. Bracey (1991), and David Berliner and Bruce J. Biddle (1995), I will limit my comments to *A Nation at Risk*, noting simply that the other commission reports mentioned above utilized very similar data to assess the quality of American education. Regarding American students' academic achievement relative to their international peers, the authors of *A Nation at Risk* relied solely on achievement test data for high school students gathered between 1964 and 1971 from the International Assessment of Educational Achievement. The composition of students who took these tests is not comparable across countries. In most countries, a small group of students attending academic high schools were tested, whereas in the United States both college-bound and terminal students at comprehensive high schools were tested. For instance, in West Germany in the early 1970s, only 9 percent of students survived until their final year in the academic high schools, and it was this group that was tested. During the same years, 75 percent of American students reached their senior year at comprehensive high schools and were eligible to take the test (Stedman & Smith, p. 91).

Regarding American students' academic achievement relative to their elders who were educated before them, the authors of *A Nation at Risk* were very selective with the data. For example, while they bemoan a slight decline in average Scholastic Aptitude Test (SAT) scores between 1963 and 1975, they neglect to mention that scores leveled out after 1975. They also neglect to mention that the socio-economic class and racial composition of SAT test-takers had diversified during the period they studied. This increased diversity of test-takers surely accounts for some of the decline in performance and is arguably a manifestation of improvements in the educational system rather than its decline (Stedman & Smith, p. 88, Berliner & Biddle, p. 18). Like SAT scores, National Assessment of Educational Progress (NEAP) scores—the most respected measure of academic achievement for K-12 students—have been flat over the last two decades but have not declined. This is perhaps a good result given the increasing socio-economic and racial diversity of school-age children in the United States since the 1960s. It is not a great result, however. As Peterson observes, the commission reports should have simply pointed out that although the educational system had maintained its level of quality in the face of recent challenges, it had not improved. Several scholarly studies of American secondary education appeared during those same years and underscored the need for careful reform (see Boyer,

1983; Goodlad, 1984; Sizer, 1984). Instead, the commission reports chose to exploit the data with crisis rhetoric and grossly misled the public as a result. However, while the scholarly integrity of the recent educational reports is questionable, their political impact—especially *A Nation at Risk*—has been remarkable. They helped create and sustain the longest period of continuous education reform in American history, right up through Clinton's human capital agenda described above.

Educational Excellence as the Dominant Policy Ideal

The guiding ideal behind this current period of school reform is educational excellence (Peterson, 1985; Passow, 1984; Jones-Wilson, 1986; Strickland, 1985). What actually constitutes educational excellence is not always clearly defined in the reform literature, but certain themes are identifiable. The central goal seems to be that American students as a whole will learn more in school—as traditionally measured by standardized achievement tests of some form—and be better prepared to enter the work-force after graduating from high school or college (Glenn, 1985; Jennings, 1987). Present reformers believe that excellence is attainable if educators raise their standards concerning the amount of time students spend in school, the curriculum they undertake, and their promotion through the system. A. Harry Passow summarizes the educational policies of what is often called the "excellence movement" in this way:

> ...setting higher requirements for high school graduation and admission to college; eliminating "soft" subjects and mandating a common core curriculum for all students; increasing requirements in mathematics, science, and foreign languages; testing achievement more regularly; lengthening the school day and the school year; and generally "getting tough" with students, teachers, and even administrators. (Passow, 1984, p. 676)

II. The Liberal Legacy
of Equality of Opportunity

*Strategic Concerns
with the Excellence Movement*

The policies of the excellence movement have been criticized on both strategic and moral grounds. Concerning the strategic dimension of recent federal educational policy, critics charge that it is not unique or innovative but is merely a replay of the educational panic and response that followed the Russians' launching of Sputnik in 1957 (Podeschi & Hackbarth, 1986; Strickland, 1985; Jones-Wilson, 1986). During the Sputnik era, aggressive educational reform was triggered by a perceived military crisis in which the nemesis was the U.S.S.R., whereas the recent crisis is an economic one and the primary challengers are Western Europe and Japan. Still, reformers in each period have emphasized educational excellence in the form of higher standards and increased accountability for both students and educators. Moreover, unlike the more subtle scholarly treatments of public schooling published during the 1980s (see Boyer, 1983; Goodlad, 1984; Sizer, 1984), the commission reports that have shaped recent educational policy focus solely on what subjects are taught in schools and how much time is spent on them. These reports treat as unproblematic givens the more important questions of how exactly these subjects are taught and what sort of learning climates characterize typical classrooms. Gretchen Guiton and Jeannie Oakes have accurately criticized this traditional model of school reform as the "more of the same" approach (1995, p. 324).

Moral Concerns
with the Excellence Movement

My main concern, however, is with the moral dimension of federal educational policy rather than the strategic dimension. On a positive note, the policies of the current movement are more inclusive than the policies of the Sputnik era. The guiding objective of Cold War educational reform was to better identify and nurture those mathematically and scientifically gifted students who could help the United States maintain technological supremacy over the Soviet Republic (Kaestle & Smith, 1982; Jennings, 1987; Strickland, 1985). Contemporary reformers, on the other hand, understand that the economic supremacy of the United States requires more than a small technological elite, and they aim to improve the academic preparation of all American students—gifted, average, and remedial. Actually, the question of whether or not the business community truly needs the "bottom third" to become educationally excellent—whether or not the lowest-skilled jobs in the service-sector in fact require such excellence—is hotly disputed. Still, for the first time in American history, certain business leaders have lobbied Congress to increase rather than decrease federal aid to programs that serve socio-economically disadvantaged students. While testifying before Congress about his company's newfound support of increasing educational expenditures for disadvantaged populations, William Woodside of the American Can Company put it this way:

> We are agreed that the quality of public schooling we provide to all our children, including disadvantaged children, will play a major role in the ability of the United States to develop a competitive economy and a strong society. Our collective appearance here today is intended to underscore the importance we attach to national efforts to provide educational

opportunities for disadvantaged and low-income children and
our specific support for the renewal of the Chapter 1 program
of federal aid for disadvantaged and low-income children.
(quoted in Jennings, 1987, p. 107)

Yet, on a less positive note, it is important to recognize the
tenuous status of programs for socio-economically disadvantaged students—such as Head Start, Chapter One, and Upward
Bound[2]—during the present reform period. As Woodside's remarks demonstrate, many business and government leaders
support programs for disadvantaged students because they
believe that these programs enhance America's future economic
viability. However, if it turns out that programs for disadvantaged students do not successfully salvage a valuable labor force
which can be effectively exploited in the international market,
then it is reasonable to expect that support for such programs
might fade away. To invoke the language of moral and political
philosophy, this posture toward programs that serve disadvantaged populations is utilitarian in nature.[3] Educational assistance for disadvantaged populations will continue as long as
there is an economic pay-off for society as a whole. Moreover, the
interests of society as a whole are defined, in actuality, by those
business and government leaders who hold economic and political power (Apple, 1986, 1992). Perhaps this over-simplifies the
situation, but it captures the moral ethos of the excellence
movement.

In summary, while the motivations that guide the present
excellence movement are more inclusive than the excellence
campaign that followed the launch of Sputnik, they are not
sufficiently egalitarian. Current policy-makers who support
educational programs for disadvantaged persons are surely
motivated in part by humanitarian impulses, but their principal
motivation derives from their belief that the disadvantaged
population is an untapped labor force. Clearly, when educational
policy is morally criticized because it is not inclusive and ignores

the interests of the disadvantaged, an assumption is being made about what is moral. It is quite possible to argue that policies that aim mainly to cultivate individual excellence are morally superior to those that emphasize equal opportunity. In the third chapter, I will support my moral preference for equality of opportunity as thoroughly as possible.

The Liberal Consensus of the 1960s and 1970s

It is often observed that educational reform occurs in cycles (Jones-Wilson, 1986; Podeschi & Hackbarth, 1986; Cookson, Jr., 1995). In between the two waves of excellence-oriented reform identified above—the Sputnik era reforms of the late 1950s and the current excellence movement that began in the early 1980s— a different ideal dominated educational policy: equality of opportunity. Upon the discovery of social inequality in the 1960s, the Johnson administration initiated a significant array of programs aimed at equalizing educational opportunities for minorities, women, and the economically disadvantaged (Pincus, 1984). Most of these programs survived and were even increased during the Nixon and Ford administrations of the late 1960s and early 1970s. While federal programs initiated during this time totaled more than thirty in number (Levin, 1977), the three programs reviewed in the note above adequately represent the egalitarian policy focus of this period.

The federal educational programs of the 1960s and 1970s reflected what Chester E. Finn, Jr. later labeled "the liberal consensus" (Finn, Jr., 1980, p. 25). Finn defined the liberal consensus in this way:

> Distilled down to its essence, the liberal consensus in American education has been characterized by a near-boundless confidence in the ability of the national government to deploy its resources in ways that reduce the educational conse-

quences of individual differences [such as race, gender, or socio-economic class]. (p. 26)

The liberal coalition of the 1960s and 1970s redefined the traditional liberal understanding of equality of opportunity. Equal opportunity had traditionally been defined in formal terms, meaning that individuals seeking educational or employment opportunities were legally protected from discrimination on the basis of irrelevant personal characteristics such as race or religion. If discrimination did not occur, the subsequent distribution of occupational and economic rewards across different social groups was not of concern. To the modern liberal coalition, however, equal opportunity required something more substantive (see also O'Neill, 1977; Galston, 1986). All persons, regardless of racial and gender identity or economic station, should actually possess equal life chances—or equal chances for educational and occupational success—rather than mere protection from discrimination. Unlike the traditional formal conception of equal opportunity—which ignores the question of how occupational outcomes are distributed if discrimination has not taken place—the substantive conception attends to the results of economic competition as a means of measuring whether or not individuals' life chances are really equal.

Assessing Equality of Educational Opportunity in Practice

It is very difficult, for obvious reasons, to determine whether or not a future-oriented concept like equality of life chances exists in a given society. The best way to operationalize—meaning to translate into measurable language—such a concept is to examine existing patterns of occupational and economic distribution for various social groups, and to extrapolate from this information an estimate of the life prospects for children of particular social backgrounds whose futures lay ahead of them.

Robert Ennis has creatively described this measurement technique as "prospective retrospection" (1976, p. 182). In Ennis' words:

> [The] long range interest for mature parties is retrospective: Did they have equal educational opportunity? For unborn and immature parties it is prospectively retrospective: Will they, when mature (or beyond), have had equal educational opportunity? (p. 183)

Equality of life chances across social groups might be assessed by using the concept of proportional representation, which means that for any desirable social position—such as matriculation in graduate school or a business or government post—the racial and gender distribution should approximate what that distribution is in the surrounding community. Another way that equality of life chances might be measured is through the concept of "statistical independence" (Milner, 1987, p. 1059), which stipulates that the occupational prospects of young persons should not be statistically related to social background characteristics such as race or socio-economic class. It is important to note that the concepts of proportional representation and statistical independence depict a single state of affairs. A society in which the occupational success of persons has no statistical relationship with social background characteristics such as race or gender is necessarily a society characterized by proportional representation. Still, the individual concepts, while describing the same reality, capture this reality in different ways. The concept of proportional representation captures the ideal egalitarian end-state: occupational and economic parity across social groups. The concept of statistical independence draws upon the common intuition that a person's life chances should not depend on factors she cannot control. Regardless of how it is conceptualized, equality of life chances is a high, even unattainable goal, and it reflects the egalitarian idealism that characterized the liberal consensus of the 1960s and 1970s. It will be noted in the fifth chapter that substantive equality of opportunity is less strictly egalitarian than the socialist ideal of equality of material condition. Still, in relation to the excellence movements which both preceded and followed the liberal educational consensus of the 1960s and 1970s, the emphasis on equality of opportunity is striking.

Before proceeding, it is important to distinguish between the meaning of the term "liberal" as it is used by Finn to describe the dominant political orientation of the 1960s and 1970s and its meaning in the Western philosophical tradition. Finn is speaking in the modern vernacular, in which liberal politics are associated with the image of the benevolent state. The benevolent state taxes citizens heavily in order to fund programs that alleviate inequalities of opportunity associated with race, gender, or socio-economic status. Modern liberals would argue that by attending to the opportunities of all individuals, rich and poor, they are in accord with the liberal tradition. Modern conservatives, in contrast, would argue that they are the ones who stand in the liberal tradition of respecting individual rights. They respect individual rights by not taxing the earnings of working persons to the degree that liberals do. This disagreement between modern liberals and conservatives is not about the legitimacy of the historic liberal tradition, but simply about two different viewpoints on what it means to carry it out. One of the central preoccupations of this project is to demonstrate that the 1960s-1970s-era liberal consensus that Finn opposed captures the humanistic ideals of its parent philosophical tradition better than its conservative counterpart; the bulk of this effort will take place in Chapter Three.

III. The Moral Priority
of Equality of Opportunity

*The Tension Between Educational Excellence
and Equality of Opportunity*

The previous discussion demonstrates that system-wide excellence and equality of opportunity have functioned as opposing ideals between which recent educational policy has vacillated. However, the actual distinctions that have been drawn between these two opposing ideals have been subtle up to this point, focusing on the underlying motivations that animate policy-making when one or the other ideal is ascendant. To demonstrate the moral differences between the excellence and equal opportunity paradigms more clearly, it is helpful to compare them from the vantage point of the individual person instead of society as a whole. At the individual level, the benign phrase "excellence for all" becomes "excellence for me." At this level, the trade-offs between promoting individual excellence and equality of opportunity become more obvious. Consider the choice between tracked and untracked classes. The educational achievement of strong students is perhaps sacrificed when they are grouped with weaker students. But equal opportunity is sacrificed if these students are separated and the difference between them is causally related to social background. Since classes cannot be tracked and untracked at the same time, the task of negotiating between individual excellence and equality of opportunity is unavoidable.[4]

The moral conflict between individual excellence—as defined by educational achievement—and equality of opportunity is a manifestation of an even more fundamental conflict that all democratic societies face: individual liberty versus social equality. To return to the previous example, advocates of tracking argue that it violates the liberty of strong students to place them in educational environments in which their academic potential is jeopardized. Consequently, besides its utilitarian intentions in which better schooling for all is advocated as the means to economic growth to be shared by all, the present excellence movement is concerned with protecting individual liberty. The very vocabulary of the excellence campaign—goals and standards, assessment and accountability, and especially competition and choice—can be understood as a reaction to the perceived federal obsession with social leveling during the time of the liberal educational consensus (Cookson, Jr., 1995). For instance, Joseph Adelson's words adequately represent the conservative reaction to the alleged leveling inclinations of the 1960s and 1970s:

> [The federal bureaucracies] know but a single thing, that thing being a distended and distorted idea of equality, distended in that it puts equality above all other values, and distorted because it has transformed the original idea of moral equality... to the idea of numerical equality, that all groups must be represented equally in all statuses. (quoted in Pincus, 1984, p. 52)

The present reign of liberty over equality began with what Laurence Iannaccone calls the "critical realignment election" of Ronald Reagan in 1980 (Iannaccone, 1987, p. 62). Not surprisingly, the excellence movement followed directly in its wake. In Iannaccone's words, liberty is "the predominant... value of the present policy era," and "excellence in education is its policy slogan" (p. 62).

The major reform documents that have framed the present period—*A Nation at Risk* (1983) and *Goals 2000* (1994)—do not face up to the challenge of reconciling the conflicting ideals of educational excellence and equality of opportunity. Instead, these documents assume what Thomas E. Schaefer has characterized as "an easy complementarity" between the two ideals and focus almost solely on excellence (1990, p. 41). The authors of *A Nation at Risk* put it this way:

> We do not believe that a public commitment to excellence and educational reform must be made at the expense of a strong public commitment to the equitable treatment of our diverse population... we cannot permit one to yield to the other either in principle or in practice. (p. 117)

Despite the egalitarian rhetoric, however, the policy recommendations of *A Nation at Risk* fail to adequately address the needs of poor, non-white, and inner-city youth. For example, no strategies are suggested to retain potential drop-outs, to stimulate job opportunities for urban adolescents, or to entice good teachers to work in inner-city schools. Similarly, Clinton's plan purports to create "a vision of excellence and equity that will guide all federal and related programs" (*Goals 2000*, p. 2),[5] yet it does not sufficiently address the catastrophic social and economic conditions in which many American children live (Cookson Jr., 1995; Kozol, 1991).

Reconciling the Tension Between Excellence and Equality of Opportunity

In the real world where educational policy is made, there is clearly no "easy complementarity" between the moral ideals of excellence and equality of opportunity. From Plato and Friedrich Nietzsche to Jean-Jacques Rousseau and John Rawls, the Western philosophical tradition is full of persuasive arguments for the primacy of either excellence or equality. Schaefer is probably correct when he observes that one's preference for excellence or equality is due to one's constitutional make-up as much as it is due to one's rational opinion. Reconciliation between the two ideals is possible; however, it surely does not suffice to simply assert that both ideals are valuable while at the same time getting on with the business of promoting excellence. This is exactly what the reports quoted above do, and their policy recommendations are morally simplistic as a result.

A substantial argument for substantive equal opportunity will be presented in the third chapter, but I wish to introduce the following thought by way of preview. Responding to Aristotle's exhortation—"it belongs to the philosopher to order"—Schaefer attempts to set excellence and equality of opportunity in order of priority. In doing so, Schaefer draws a helpful distinction between metaphysical and temporal priority. Schaefer acknowledges—as did both Rousseau and Rawls—that the ideal of equality is metaphysically parasitic. That is, it depends upon other values, such as liberty or excellence, for its meaning (see also Gutmann, 1980, p. 10). For instance, the concept of equal liberty is important because of the moral value of liberty. At the same time, however, Schaefer argues that equal opportunity should be temporally prioritized over liberty or excellence. Until equality of opportunity is secured in society, those that succeed cannot claim comparative superiority with assurance, for it is always possible that their success is merely the product of fortunate circumstances. To summarize: "Equality for what?" is, for Schaefer, the important question, and his answer is "equality for excellence" (1990, p. 49).

IV. Introduction to the Book

The Purposes of the Project

The previous discussion surveyed recent federal educational policy with the intent of clarifying its underlying purposes. If we look backward through the last decade and a half, in which the policy emphasis was mainly on individual and system-wide excellence in the service of national economic objectives, we discover a prior legacy of equality of opportunity. As stated above, the liberal educational program of the 1960s and 1970s—related to the larger, liberal political philosophical tradition but not identical with it—emphasized substantive equality of opportunity rather than merely formal equality. The formal interpretation of equal opportunity requires only the absence of barriers to educational and employment opportunities, such as selection procedures that discriminate against persons based on irrelevant factors like racial or gender identity. The more substantive interpretation looks at occupational and economic results, and assesses the actual life chances for individuals in various social groups. The central purposes of this project are to promote the substantive conception of equality of educational opportunity, to identify certain populations of children who would be the primary beneficiaries of a re-commitment to substantive equal educational opportunity, and to examine the policy implications of this commitment at the federal and state levels.

The Perspective Advanced in the Project

I will say more about equal opportunity as the project unfolds, but some historical background is helpful here in order to introduce my theoretical perspective. To begin with, the concept of equal opportunity has its origin in the liberal political philosophical tradition, in which the primary subject of political theory is the individual rather than society as a whole. Individuals, liberals assume, have a fundamental interest in liberty—in pursuing their own rational plans without interference from the state. Yet, there is also an equality assumption in the liberal tradition. All persons, by virtue of being human, possess equal rights to liberty. One person's exercise of liberty cannot impede that of another. Different varieties of liberalism gain their identity through how they define liberty and equality, and how they propose that these frequently oppositional value commitments should be reconciled in actual societies. Under the liberal model, each individual in society possesses a right to educational and social opportunities that are roughly equivalent with others. Further, liberals have traditionally believed that social and economic rewards should accrue to individuals on the basis of performance, rather than on the basis of birthright. The assumption is that individuals should earn their rewards, and that the function of the equal opportunity principle is to ensure that the race is as fair as possible. In this way, the principle of equality of opportunity is a meritocratic principle. For the greater part of this book, I will adopt the traditional, liberal, meritocratic perspective.

I should clarify immediately that I am using the term meritocracy in a positive sense, where educational and occupational competition is truly fair because substantial efforts are made to correct for socio-economic hardships that prevent poor children from demonstrating their potential. In an authentic meritocracy, talented individuals from all classes would rise to important positions because inequalities of birth would be mitigated by egalitarian social programs of some type. Yet certain social theorists, such as Michael Young, John Schaar, and Rawls, use the term meritocracy negatively rather than positively. For these theorists, authentic meritocracies are even harsher than aristocracies for those under-talented persons who "lose" in the competitive market even when the conditions are fair. Since a person's talents are at least partly a matter of pure fortune, the material well-being of these persons should be protected regardless of their ability to compete successfully in the market. A liberal theory of justice, these theorists assert, must protect the interests of the under-talented for the simple reason that they are human beings. According to this perspective, equality of opportunity operates a little more abstractly than it does in the traditional perspective. All persons deserve more than an equal opportunity to compete for social and economic goods. Indeed, all persons deserve an equal opportunity to lead satisfying lives regardless of their native gifts. I will be more specific about my own interpretation of meritocratic equal opportunity as I proceed, but it is important to remember that not all liberals support the meritocratic interpretation of equality of opportunity.

Regarding educational opportunity specifically, three additional clarifications are necessary. First, the main distinction between equal educational opportunity and equal occupational opportunity is that the former exists in an instrumental relationship with the latter. Educational attainment, typically defined as the number of years of schooling a person has completed, is directly related to occupational success. As Max Weber (1948) observed earlier this century, and Randall Collins (1971, 1979) more recently confirmed, educational attainment is highly correlated with occupational status or prestige. Speaking of the relationship between educational attainment and earnings, M. Blaug (1972) observes that "the universality of [the] positive association between education and earnings is one of the most striking findings of modern social science" (p. 54; see also Psacharopoulos, 1975; Psacharopoulos & Tilak, 1992; Jencks, 1985). Second, the concept of educational opportunity is being interpreted here in the most expansive sense possible. What is envisioned is the total set of educative influences on children, including family and community as well as schooling influences (see Strike, 1988, p. 158). It will be argued in Chapter Four that this totalist conception has been implicit in the American conception of educational opportunity from the beginning. Third, given this expansive conception, it is obvious that perfect equality of educational opportunity is merely a guiding ideal. In Charles Frankel's words, this ideal implies "a direction of effort, not a goal to be achieved" (Frankel, 1971, p. 209). The moral issue concerning equal educational opportunity is not whether or not we fulfill it completely, but whether or not we are sufficiently close.

A Rationale for the Project

Before proceeding to preview the remaining chapters, I wish to articulate four reasons why the subject of this book—equality of educational opportunity—is uniquely inviting for philosophical exploration. First, philosophy is most accessible when it attends to what Charles Taylor has called "commonsense understandings," the ideas or ideals that are widely shared by a particular community (Taylor, 1983, p. 62). Equality of opportunity, the parent concept from which equal educational opportunity derives, is just such an ideal. It is without rival the dominant conception of distributive justice in the American mind (Kymlicka, 1990; Schaar, 1967; Frankel, 1971; Fishkin, 1983). John Schaar, in what is now recognized as a classic critique of equality of opportunity as a social ideal, describes its ubiquity in this way:

> So pervasive and habitual is this way of thinking today that it is virtually impossible to criticize it with any hope of persuading others of its weaknesses. One is not dealing with a set of specific propositions logically arrayed, but with an atmospheric condition, a climate of opinion that unconsciously governs articulate thought in a variety of fields. (1967, p. 238)[6]

The next two reasons why the subject of equal opportunity is philosophically inviting flow from the first. Second, as Frankel has observed, "the universal popularity of an idea usually discourages its close inspection... [and] should arouse some suspicion." Frankel continues:

> If equality of opportunity is a significant ideal, there ought to be some people who are opposed to it. Or it may well be that it is a highly stretchable or ambiguous concept, which cloaks strongly divergent ideas over which people do in fact dis-

agree... The peace it brings is therefore an unstable peace and one that comes at too high a price. (1971, p. 192)

Frankel is correct; equality of opportunity is, in fact, a highly stretchable concept, encompassing many divergent interpretations while creating the illusion of consensus. One of the primary missions of philosophers is to expose disagreement where agreement has been assumed. In the case of equal opportunity, the ground is fertile. Third, given our unconscious habituation to the ideal of equal opportunity and our corresponding acceptance of the illusion of consensus that it confers, it is not surprising that equality of opportunity is forgotten during certain periods of history. As the previous review of the excellence movement in education indicates, Americans are currently in one of these periods. It is very important that policy-makers are reminded of an ideal they claim to hold—an ideal which has become so familiar to them as to be almost ineffectual.

The final reason why the subject of equal opportunity is philosophically inviting is the most compelling. Human lives are at stake. If equality of opportunity—by any reasonable interpretation—does not exist in a given society, then those persons without sufficient opportunities will suffer. I will argue in the next chapter that educational opportunities in the United States are quite unequal, and children suffer as a result. Indeed, more than one observer has labeled the present distribution of educational opportunities in America "a national disgrace" (Slavin, 1994, p. 98; see also Cookson, Jr, 1995; Kozol, 1991). Educational philosophers must not ignore problems like this if they are to earn their keep. Education needs more loyal critics like Jonathan Kozol, who, in *Savage Inequalities* (1991), calls America to account regarding its self-perception as the land of opportunity. I will define the concept of educational opportunity more broadly than does Kozol—who focuses on financial resources available to rich and poor school districts—but I share his premise that present opportunities are "savagely" unequal.

V. Preview
of the Remaining Chapters

The central purposes of this chapter were twofold. First, I introduced two ideals that have animated federal educational policy-making over the last forty years, equality of opportunity in the 1960s and 1970s and excellence from the early 1980s until the present. Second, I made an initial plea for revitalizing our nation's commitment to equality of educational opportunity, or, more specifically, the substantive interpretation of equal educational opportunity. The substantive interpretation emphasizes equality of life chances across social groups, as opposed to the mere absence of discrimination. Unlike the formal conception of equal opportunity, the substantive conception attends to the results of occupational and economic competition as a means of assessing whether or not the life chances of individuals in different social groups are truly equal.

Whereas this first chapter was a mixture of political and philosophical analysis, the following three chapters will be more distinct in their methodological approaches. The second chapter is sociological in method, in which I attempt to explain the processes by which certain demographically identifiable student populations experience disproportionate failure rates in school. It is these students who would be the primary beneficiaries of a national re-commitment to substantive equality of educational opportunity. The third chapter is philosophical in method, in which I attempt to justify my commitment to substantive equality of educational opportunity by connecting this commitment to certain valuable aspects of the historic liberal tradition in political philosophy. The fourth chapter deals with educational politics, where I examine the ways in which federal and state-level policy-makers have historically defined and operationalized equality of educational opportunity. In Chapter Five, I will make some broad policy recommendations based on the preceding discussions, and close the book by arguing that equality of opportunity, and by extension equality of educational opportunity, resonates with our deepest intuitions concerning the most equitable organization of societies. Finally, I want to clarify that although the project as a whole is multi-disciplinary in approach and intended to contribute to the academic field known as Foundations of Education, its conceptual and rhetorical core is philosophical. The project is motivated by my attraction to substantive equality of opportunity as a moral ideal—as introduced above and outlined in Chapter Three—and the surrounding chapters simply address the many questions that arise concerning how this ideal might be applied in practice.

Notes

1. Human capital is an economic term which refers to the productive capacities of individuals or the work-force as a whole. Human capital theorists assert that formal education makes workers more productive, and therefore fuels the national economy. However, while the connection between formal education and on-the-job productivity occupies almost common sense status in the public mind, it has never been clearly demonstrated empirically (Berliner, 1995).
2. Project Head Start was initiated in 1965 with the objective of increasing the academic readiness of pre-school age children in impoverished areas. Chapter One—officially known as Title One—was established as part of the Elementary and Secondary Education Act of 1965, and established compensatory programs for low-income elementary and secondary students. The Upward Bound program is operated mainly by colleges and universities and attempts to prepare under-achieving high-school students for entrance into postsecondary education of some type.
3. Utilitarian social policies aim to maximize the level of "utility"—

typically equated with material wealth and security—that accrues to members of society taken as a whole. If the wealth of society as a whole is maximized, utilitarians reason, then by definition the wealth of the average person in society is maximized. For utilitarians, this is as close as can be morally expected to securing the economic rights of individuals.

4. The claims above are worded the way they are to illustrate the trade-off between individual excellence and equal opportunity. Regarding tracking, the balance of the research actually suggests that above-average students are not negatively affected by placement in heterogeneous classrooms (Oakes, Gamoran, & Page, 1992; Gamoran & Berends, 1987; Slavin, 1987, 1990), although gifted students are perhaps hindered (Kulick & Kulick, 1987). Regarding the correlational relationship between social background and school success, the research clearly demonstrates that it exists (see Miller, 1995; Bennett & LeCompte, 1990).

5. The term "equity" can be treated as a synonym of equality of opportunity. As Amartya Sen (1992) points out, most social systems are supported by the claim that they hold something equal; the important question is "Equality of what?" In this book, I argue that individual opportunity, or life prospects, is the important variable to be held equal, as opposed to absolute economic freedoms, social conditions, or something else. Equality of opportunity means sameness of opportunity, a similar chance to succeed. Hopefully, the similarity between this concept and the notion of equity, or fairness, is evident.

6. As the term implies, distributive justice refers to the degree of justice, or fairness, that characterizes a particular community's system of distributing social and economic rewards to its members. The term is distinct from retributive justice, which has to do with the fairness with which retribution, or punishment, is assigned to members of society who break the rules.

Chapter Two

Less Than Equal:
The Chronic Victims
of Inequality
of Educational Opportunity

I. Chapter Preview

My guiding objective in this chapter is to identify several social background characteristics that are statistically correlated with academic failure, and then to give some reasons why students who possess certain of these attributes often experience difficulties in school. While I will advance what I call an interactionist perspective which recognizes that both environmentally related characteristics of children and problematic schooling practices play a role in producing unequal academic outcomes across social groups, I must also directly address the controversial dissenting view that genetically determined group differences in intelligence are the primary cause. After trying to explain the causes of the educational difficulties of certain groups, I will attach a human face to the social tragedy of unequal educational opportunity by presenting a portrait of an educationally disadvantaged young man. The intended effect of this portrait is to communicate the profound importance of equal educational opportunity for individual persons. Finally, it is essential that I explicitly relate the discussion of the educational struggles of certain groups of children to my larger concern with substantive equality of educational opportunity. My central concern in this project is not with inequality of educational outcomes across social groups itself, but rather with entrenched social inequalities that make such inequality predictable from the start.

II. Five Social Background Characteristics Associated With School Failure

It is important to understand as much as possible about students who are struggling in school so that educators and policy-makers might discover ways they can better serve these children. A knowledge of who it is that needs the most assistance is also helpful because resources are scarce, and there is a political need to direct these resources to those who need them most. In *Schooling Disadvantaged Children: Racing Against Catastrophe* (1990), Gary Natriello et al. discuss five social background characteristics that are most strongly correlated with academic failure. Before addressing these background attributes, however, three crucial qualifications are necessary. First and foremost, these characteristics are only to be understood as gross indicators because they merely indicate that there is a statistical tendency for students who possess one or more of them to experience academic failure (p. 14). These statistical correlations do not in themselves explain the processes by which many students who possess one or more of the identified attributes come to experience academic difficulty. Second, these correlations are not even close to absolute; many students demonstrate great resiliency and beat the odds. Finally, these indicators are fluid; students may possess many of these characteristics at one time and not at another.

1. Race and Ethnicity

Race and ethnicity is perhaps the best known correlate with educational disadvantagement. Historically, members of minority groups have not succeeded at the same level as white students. Black and Hispanic youth have particularly high rates of academic failure. Regarding educational achievement—typically measured by standardized test scores and school grades—the results of the 1985 *National Assessment of Educational Progress (NAEP)* show that the reading, writing, and mathematics skills of black and Hispanic children are substantially below those of white children. Regarding educational attainment—years of schooling completed—the 1986 *Current Population Survey* (Bruno, 1988) concludes that 13.9 percent of whites between 22 and 24 years of age are neither enrolled in school nor possess high school diplomas, compared with 17.3 percent of blacks and 38.2 percent of Hispanics. However, it is important to acknowledge that these studies lump all black and Hispanic subgroups into unities, obscuring the fact that there is great diversity of school success and failure within these broad racial categories (Ogbu, 1987). For example, less than one-half of Mexican Americans between the ages of 25 and 34 have finished high school, whereas more than four-fifths of Americans of Cuban ancestry have completed high school (U.S. Bureau of the Census, 1988a). It is also important to clarify immediately that racial and ethnic identity is conceived here as a socially constructed handicap, not a natural or genetic handicap. The position that race is a socially constructed handicap in relation to academic achievement is not without dissenters (Jenson, 1969, 1973; Herrnstein, 1971, 1973; Herrnstein & Murray, 1994). Yet, while the arguments of these dissenters will be addressed below, the social constructivist thesis will be defended (see Gould, 1981; Lewontin, 1984; Appiah, 1992).

2. Poverty

Data pertaining to the correlation between poverty and educational achievement is scarce, but it has been demonstrated that nine-year-old children from advantaged urban families score nearly one standard deviation higher in reading assessments than nine-year-old children from disadvantaged urban families (Applebee, 1988). Regarding educational attainment, children from families living above the poverty line are almost one-half less likely to be retained in a grade than children from families living below the poverty line (Bianchi, 1984). Grade retention is both an indicator of present difficulty and a predictor of later difficulties. Children who are retained in a grade are substantially more likely to drop out of school than those who are never retained (Pallas, 1986; Sherman, 1987). Also, the *High School and Beyond Study*, which traces the educational attainment of students who were high school sophomores in 1980 (Sebring et al., 1987), reveals that 24 percent of the poorest one-fifth of sophomores in the study have not completed high school, whereas only 11 percent of the other four-fifths of sophomores have dropped out of school (Stedman et al., 1988). Finally, poverty is highly correlated with race in our society. Only 12 percent of whites live below the poverty line, while 46 percent of blacks and 40 percent of Hispanics live below the poverty line (U.S. Bureau of the Census, 1988c).

3. Single-Parent Families

Analysis of the 1986 *NAEP* shows that, by the third grade, the reading skills of children from single-parent homes are at least one full year behind children from two-parent homes (Natriello et al., 1990). Differences of similar magnitude are found concerning mathematics proficiency. Data from the *High School and*

Beyond Study demonstrates that children from single-parent homes are almost twice as likely to drop out of high school (22.4 percent drop out) as children from two-parent homes (12 percent) (Stedman et al., 1988). Family structure is correlated with both racial identity and poverty. Approximately three-fifths of black children and more than one-third of Hispanic children live in single-parent homes, whereas less than one-fifth of white children live with only one parent (U.S. Bureau of the Census, 1989). Seventy-three percent of children who spend part of their childhood in a single-parent household live in poverty at least part of that time, while children from a two-parent household have only a 20 percent chance of living in poverty (for one year or more) before their tenth year (Ellwood, 1988).

4. Poorly Educated Mothers

At every age, children of under-educated mothers lag behind children of educated mothers in educational achievement. On the 1986 *NAEP*, third graders with mothers who have finished high school scored approximately six-tenths of a standard deviation higher overall than those with mothers who have not completed high school (Natriello et al., 1990). Regarding educational attainment, students with mothers who have completed high school are two to three times less likely to drop out of school than those with mothers who have not finished school (Barro & Kolstad, 1987, from the *High School and Beyond Study*). The level of education of a child's mother is also highly correlated with race: 13 percent of white children have mothers with no high school degree, while 30 percent of black children and more than 50 percent of Hispanic children have mothers with no degree (U.S. Bureau of the Census, 1988b).

5. Limited-English Proficiency

Limited-English proficiency (LEP) makes it difficult for students to perform in American classrooms regardless of the subject being taught, whether it be mathematics, science, or the more language intensive subjects such as language arts and social studies. Data from the 1986 *NAEP* suggest that the English and mathematics skills of third graders who have been exposed to a language other than English in their homes are approximately one-half year behind students whose only exposure has been to the English language. For students who have no exposure to English at home, the difference is closer to one full year (Natriello et al.). Moreover, students from homes in which a non-English language is spoken are more than twice as likely to drop out of school as students from homes where only English is spoken (Salganik and Celebuski, 1987).

Correlations between Attributes

As described above, racial and ethnic identity is correlated with each of the other four attributes discussed above. Also, poverty is correlated not only with race and ethnicity, but with the other three characteristics of educational disadvantagement as well. For example, as mentioned above, children from single-parent homes are more likely to be poor than children from two-parent homes. Further, families with poorly educated mothers or families with limited English proficiency suffer higher rates of poverty than families that do not share these characteristics. The fact that the third, fourth, and fifth variables are all correlated with the first two reveals the complex, multi-dimensional web of social handicaps that racial and ethnic-minority and poor children have to conquer in order to succeed in school. For the sake of simplicity and clarity, however, the following discussion will attend mainly to the educational experiences of poor and minority children.

III. An Historical Introduction to Causal Explanations for Educational Disadvantagement

The Cultural Deprivation Thesis of the 1950s and 1960s

While it is important to identify those ascriptive social background characteristics of children that are most commonly associated with academic difficulty, the discussion cannot stop there. As stated above, the discovery of correlations between these background characteristics and educational failure tells policy-makers and educators nothing about why these correlations exist, or how they might reverse these patterns. As a way of introducing the question of causation, it is helpful to briefly review the major explanations for what scholars call "educational disadvantagement" advanced over the last four decades.

Most researchers who studied educational disadvantagement in the 1950s and 1960s assumed that the causes of the disproportionate academic failure rates of ethnic-minority and poor children were best explained by certain deficits that these children carried with them to school. One highly controversial version of this perspective, which Carl Bereiter (1985) described as a "central deficit" explanation, was that poor children, particularly black children, were simply less intelligent on average than their wealthier, white peers for reasons related to genetics rather than to their environment (Jensen, 1969, 1973; Herrnstein, 1971, 1973). Richard J. Herrnstein and Charles Murray recently re-asserted this genetic explanation of educational disadvantagement in *The Bell Curve* (1994), which will be addressed later in this chapter. The majority of researchers, however, emphasized environmental over genetic reasons for high failure rates on the part of minority and lower-class students. According to the mainstream perspective, the academic struggles of these students were best explained by theories of cultural deprivation, which maintained that disadvantaged children grow up in what Oscar Lewis called a "culture of poverty" (1966, p. 19), which fails to nurture those linguistic and analytical skills that are essential for academic success (Hunt, 1964; Havighurst, 1965; Lewis, 1966; Brooks, 1966). As part of its investigation into the causes of the Watts Riots in 1965, the McCone Commission report articulated this position quite clearly:

> Children in disadvantaged areas are often deprived in the pre-school years of the necessary foundations for learning. They have not had the full range of experiences so necessary to the development of language in the pre-school years, and hence they are poorly prepared to learn when they enter school.... The Commission concludes that this is the major reason for low achievement in the disadvantaged areas. (quoted in Hurn, 1993, p. 151)

It is important to note that the usage of the cultural deprivation label went far beyond what the originators of the term intended. The term was originally meant to describe a limited population of very poor, inner-city children, but many scholars and policy-makers began to use the term to describe poor children—or, even more inappropriately, black children—in general (Hurn, 1993). Even careful scholars employed the popular term because of its currency in popular discourse, despite personal reservations. For instance, Frank Reissman titled his study of educational disadvantagement *The Culturally Deprived Child* (1962), fully knowing that the cultures of the impoverished populations he was examining were more appropriately described as different than as deficient, a perspective described below (Friedman, 1970).

The Cultural Difference Thesis
of the 1960s and 1970s

Cultural difference theories arose in the 1960s and 1970s as reactions to cultural deprivation theories (see Baratz & Baratz, 1970; Clark, 1965, 1972; Valentine, 1968, 1971). Cultural difference theorists argued that cultural deprivation theories, by locating the causes of educational disadvantagement in children's experiences prior to and outside of their school experiences, allow educators to place all the responsibility for academic failure on students. Cultural difference theorists did the opposite. They charged that schools are to blame for the high academic failure rates of certain populations, and focused their attention on children's struggles during school. As the name implies, the basic thesis of this perspective was that disadvantaged children were not educationally shortchanged by their home cultures, but that these cultures simply did not match up well with the dominant white, middle-class culture valued in schools. They argued that schools produce academic failure in educationally disadvantaged youth because they fail to build upon the existing knowledge bases that these students carry into their schools, knowledge bases that are different from mainstream students but perfectly legitimate. Indeed, Stephen Baratz and Joan Baratz went so far as to contend that the school system's failure to value the existing knowledge bases of disadvantaged students was a manifestation of "institutional racism" (1970, p. 30). One central issue about which cultural difference and cultural deficit thinkers disagreed is still with us today in the form of the Ebonics controversy. Echoing the pro-Ebonics position advanced years later, some cultural difference theorists argued that black-English was not grammatically deficient, but simply a legitimate variant of English that was systematically devalued in schools. As Baratz and Baratz put it: "Speaking standard English is a linguistic disadvantage for the black youth on the streets of Harlem. A disadvantage created by a difference is not the same thing as a deficit" (p. 36).

The Interactionist Synthesis of the Present-Day

The historical evolution of explanations for educational disadvantagement is a clear example of Georg Friedrich Hegel's great insight regarding the development of social knowledge. Early cultural deprivation theories provided a thesis to which cultural difference theories were an antithesis. Over time, a superior, interactionist approach arose which synthesized these opposing theories (Rist, 1977; Richardson et al., 1989; Hurn, 1993; Natriello et al., 1990). The interactionist approach avoids locating the sole causes of academic failure exclusively in either student characteristics or in the incompetence of schools. Although advocates of the interactionist perspective lament that Lewis' observation concerning a culture of poverty was inappropriately generalized to certain ethnic-minority and poor populations as whole groups, they do acknowledge that chronically impoverished, socially isolated inner-city or rural families often fail to nurture the nascent intellectual capabilities of their young. At the same time, however, advocates of the interactionist view acknowledge that a predominantly white, middle-class teaching force is under-prepared to build upon the knowledge and abilities that racial and ethnic-minority and poor children do bring to the classroom, and that certain traditional schooling practices unnecessarily exacerbate learning gaps between these students and their more privileged counterparts. In other words, both the cultural deprivation theorists and the cultural difference theorists were partly right, and any reasonable solutions to the problem of educational disadvantagement must address both problems that originate outside schools—such as poverty, racism, or social dysfunction—and problems that are caused by the schooling experience itself.

Another Theoretical Scheme: Functional Versus Conflict-Oriented Explanations of Educational Disadvantagement

The historical debate about whether cultural deprivation or cultural difference is the proper explanatory lense for understanding educational disadvantagement was one particular instance of a larger, ongoing debate concerning the degree to which schools are meritocratic institutions. Actually, the debate between what Christopher Hurn (1993) labels the "functionalist" and the "conflict" perspectives on schooling has addressed very large questions about the actual importance of education in the modern world of work and the efficacy of schooling for providing skills that modern jobs require, in addition to the question about whether schools are authentically fair sorting machines that match graduates to jobs that fit their cognitive skill-levels (see Clark, 1961; Bowles & Gintis, 1976; Meyer, 1977; Collins, 1971, 1979). Only the last question crosses our purposes here, however, and, like the previous two, the functionalists have answered in the positive and the conflict theorists have answered in the negative.

Advocates of the traditional view that American schools successfully serve their meritocratic "function" found support in the status attainment research of the 1970s, one aspect of which attended to secondary schools specifically (see Sewell & Hauser, 1976; Alexander et al., 1975; Jencks, 1979). Essentially, the education-related aspect of this research attempted to assess the relative power of the purely ascriptive variable of students' socioeconomic status versus measured intelligence as a determinant of success in high school and higher education. The relevant question regarding the meritocratic status of schooling concerned the degree to which teachers consciously or unconsciously favor students who think and act in ways that accord with middle-class culture. Assuming that measures of intelligence, or I.Q., do tell us something useful about a person's cognitive abilities, the consistent outcome of these studies was that when intelligence is controlled for, social class is a very weak predictor of educational success. Intelligence, on the contrary—at least as measured by tests given to high school freshman—was found to be the strongest single predictor of students' future grades and educational attainment when social class was held constant. Consequently, while many functionalists admitted that socio-economic contingencies are likely related to a family's ability to intellectually nurture children, they have argued that this problem lies beyond schools, and that secondary teachers as a whole are not guilty of cultural favoritism, or worse yet, racism.

Upon close analysis, the evidence from the status attainment research of the 1970s cannot support a broad functionalist claim for a meritocratic school system. It is true that cognitive ability—along with future aspirations, which were not mentioned above—exercises a far greater independent impact on high school and college success than does social class, meaning that poor and minority students with high I.Q.s and aspirations are not handicapped at this stage by social background characteristics beyond their control. However, one fatal flaw of the status attainment research is that it measured cognitive ability at age fourteen, and it is entirely possible, even probable, that the way in which students of different cultural groups experience schooling prior to reaching high school accounts for much of their differences in I.Q. measured at this time. Recognizing this possibility, many conflict-oriented researchers have turned to primary schooling in order to assess the impact that cultural differences have on children's schooling experiences. Along with this shift in focus, a strict reliance on quantitative, survey-driven methodology has given way to more qualitative, observational methods, as researchers have tried to open the black box of schooling in hopes of understanding its inner workings rather than merely determining its most general effects. While I do not subscribe to the more vindictive explanations of educational disadvantagement advocated by Baratz and Baratz, in which teachers are painted as a mono-cultural group of villains, or at least incompetents, I do share the conflict theorists' general suspicion that traditional primary schooling practices are at least partially responsible for the disproportionate failure rates of poor and ethnic-minority students.

IV. A Culture-Centered Interactionist Explanation of Educational Disadvantagement

The Under-Preparation of Poor Students For School

As an advocate of the interactionist approach to understanding the causes of educational disadvantagement, I depart from the strict cultural difference approach because I assume that poor and minority students often arrive at school physically, socially, and intellectually under-prepared. The inability of chronically impoverished families to adequately prepare their children for school is neither surprising nor shameful. For example, having lost their husbands to despair and surrender, many African-American women are raising families on their own and are working long hours at low-paying jobs to make ends meet. It is difficult to nurture a child's mind when one is either on the job or sleeping. For those without jobs, the American safety net does not provide much. Many families cannot provide their children with adequate food and health care—which remains a privilege and not a right despite Clinton's legislative efforts in 1993—much less with books or educational outings that condition their minds for learning (see Miller, 1995). Still, these hardships are related to broad social inequalities, and in some cases pathologies, of which schooling only plays one part, and the cultural difference theorists' tendency to blame schools for unequal outcomes across social groups captures only half of the truth. Having offered this qualifier, however, I will now focus on this very half: the way in which culturally-influenced interactions between poor and minority children and the educators that serve them often contribute to academic failure on the part of these students. I will return to an explicit discussion of broader social problems when I make some policy recommendations in the final chapter.

Three further qualifications are necessary before proceeding. First, while it might appear to some that I make educators the primary villains, this is not my intent; the vast majority of educators in this country are quite well-intentioned and often work heroically under difficult conditions. However, the broader American culture that schools reflect is not very inclusive, and even good-hearted teachers get caught as mediators between a dominating culture and certain disenfranchised populations. Second, I do not intend to imply that schools are completely mono-cultural, middle-class institutions. Although teaching seems like the quintessential middle-class occupation, many teachers have grown up in working-class families (Alexander, et al., 1987), and about ten percent of America's teaching force is non-white (American Association of Colleges for Teacher Education, 1989). Still, the discussion below will address the cultural complexities that arise when a predominantly white, middle-class teaching force encounters a student population that is becoming progressively less white and middle-class, due to the "white flight" phenomenon in recent decades and also to longer-term demographic changes in the youth population as a whole. Finally, while not all of the researchers cited below studied elementary-age children specifically, the fact is that children's educational fates are largely determined by their first six to eight years of formal schooling, and I believe these years deserve the most attention. In order to make the text below less cumbersome, I am going to use the term "non-mainstream" to describe both ethnic-minority and low-income children. This term is meant to capture the marginalization that many of these children experience in school as a result of culturally-influenced interactions with their teachers that impact them in negative ways.

Cultural Congruence as "Capital" for Mainstream Students

As stated above, the cultural conventions that characterize American schools—communication, behavior, work-ethic, and even relaxation conventions—are largely middle-class in nature (Persell, 1977; Delpit, 1988; Hurn, 1993). As a result, middle-class children who encounter similar cultural styles in their homes and neighborhoods enjoy an advantage over their non-mainstream peers who spend their pre-school years in very different environments. For example, the knowledge schemata of middle-class children generally matches standard primary school curricula more closely than lower-class children. Also, middle-class children are more likely to be used to the question and answer style of teaching that is common in schools (Brice-Heath, 1982). Even subtle differences such as habitually holding someone's gaze when listening benefit middle-class children who see this modeled in their homes (Byers & Byers, 1972). Pierre Bourdieu and Jean-Claude Passeron describe the cultural familiarity that ethnic-majority and middle-class children enjoy—and often convert into academic success—as "cultural capital" (1977).

Cultural Incongruity as "Foreign Currency" for Non-Mainstream Students

In contrast to cultural capital, the cultural styles that non-mainstream children carry into school are described by Bourdieu and Passeron as "foreign currency." Not surprisingly, this foreign currency converts not into academic success, but academic failure. Non-mainstream children often are unable to demonstrate their intelligence to middle-class teachers, some of whom tend to evaluate academic and behavioral performance in ethnocentric ways. For instance, Ray McDermott refers to "communicative code differences" between white elementary school teachers and non-mainstream students—differences in dialect, patterns of body movement, and verbal interaction rhythms—which can cause misunderstanding on both sides (1987, p. 174). In some cases, teachers can work out cultural differences with their children. However, cultural assumptions are deeply ingrained by adulthood, and teachers' work-loads are very demanding. Consequently, many teachers do not take the time.

Two qualifications are necessary. First, all social groups possess culture, but cultural capital is restricted to those resources which are defined with reference to a particular social group that dominates the powerful and privileged positions in a society (Collins, 1979). Second, to say that what counts as cultural capital is defined by a dominant social group is not to say that such capital remains within the sole possession of the dominant group over time. Several recent studies have shown that behaviors associated with cultural capital such as those listed above are less perfectly correlated with traditional measures of socio-economic status—such as father's educational attainment and head of household's occupation—than has been typically assumed (Crouse et al., 1979; Sewell & Hauser, 1976; Portes & Wilson, 1976).

Further Examples of Cultural Incongruity
Between Schools and Non-Mainstream Students

I have provided a few concrete examples concerning the abstract claim that the culture of schooling is foreign to many non-mainstream children, but it is important to demonstrate this claim more completely. Following L. Scott Miller's (1995) and Roland G. Tharp's (1989) more comprehensive discussions, I will provide three brief illustrations regarding the schooling experiences of native Hawaiians and blacks, two ethnic groups that experience disproportionate rates of academic failure. One illustration of the cultural mismatch thesis concerns the social organization of classroom learning, which in American public schools typically means one teacher in front of a large group of children providing information to them through lecture and assessing their comprehension through asking them questions (Goodlad, 1984; Sizer, 1984), although this pattern is not without exceptions. This mode of teaching and learning does not come naturally for many native Hawaiian children, who come from a kinship-oriented culture in which they learn many skills and concepts by working collaboratively with their siblings, seeking advice from their elders only when necessary (Tharp, 1982). The teacher-centered, individualistic mode of teaching and learning also places a strain on many African-American children, who also seem to need more peer interaction, and more variation in learning tasks, than their middle-class, white peers (Morgan, 1990; Boykin, 1982).

Another illustration of the cultural mismatch thesis concerns classroom discourse issues, such as patterns of questioning and even language itself. Regarding the former, I cited Shirley Brice-Heath's (1982) research above, which compared questioning styles employed by parents in middle-class white and working-class black homes. In Brice-Heath's study, middle-class white parents tended to address their questions to individual children and asked specific questions about people, objects, and places, whereas working-class black parents tended to ask open-ended analogy-type questions such as "What is this like?" While the latter type of questions undoubtedly cultivate creativity in children, it is the former type of questions that children generally encounter in primary school, and middle-class white children are better prepared to answer their teachers than their working-class black peers. Brice-Heath's study did not address the questioning styles used by middle-class black parents, but these styles are likely a hybrid of the styles used by middle-class whites and working-class blacks. As for native Hawaiian children, the questioning styles they experience at home is more similar to working-class blacks than the dominant middle-class style they encounter at school (Jordan, 1985). Finally, the hardships that limited-English proficient (LEP) children face in American classrooms is almost too obvious to mention, but is more pervasive an obstacle than anything mentioned thus far. As noted above, LEP status is one of the main predictors of educational under-performance, and the constant funding battles over English-as-a-Second-Language (ESL) and bilingual programs reflect the importance of the issue. The advantage of middle-class white children in respect to language compatibility cannot be over-stated.

One final illustration concerns dominant teaching and learning styles (or cognitive styles), which have their roots in historic class-related differences between social groups in access to formal schooling, but then manifest themselves in ways that high-status and low-status cultures think and learn. Formal educational institutions typically promote two broad types of learning styles: an analytic style that cultivates the ability to break complex ideas and skills into discrete parts, and what Miller calls a "verbal" style, which cultivates the ability to explain things out loud and on paper (p. 254). Since the Western approach to schooling is to gather large numbers of children together in a room and then to teach them about their world, the corresponding approach to teaching and learning is abstract and de-contextualized by definition. This approach to schooling leads to an over-emphasis on analysis and verbal communication. Because whites have experienced much more formal schooling on average than either native Hawaiians or blacks, they are generally better skilled than these other cultures at thinking in ways that schools value and reward. As parents, middle-class whites—on average, again—tend to pass these learning styles on to their children almost unconsciously, and these children enjoy a competitive advantage in school situations as a result (Tharp, 1982).

The Effects of Cultural Incongruity on Teachers' Expectations of Non-Mainstream Students

As culturally-influenced miscommunications between middle-class teachers and non-mainstream children recur over time, many teachers begin to believe—usually unconsciously—that these children are academically inferior (Persell, 1977, 1993). As Christopher Hurn puts it, many bright minority and poor students are misperceived as "dull, plodding, and (at best) merely earnest" (1993, p. 197). Surely, well-intentioned teachers try to base their expectations for incoming students on "objective" information such as past grades, test scores, and narrative evaluations. But these information sources are all contaminated to some degree by middle-class cultural biases, and tend to confirm teachers' suspicions that non-mainstream students are inferior (Knapp & Woolverton, 1995). This is important because teachers' low expectations concerning the academic abilities of non-mainstream children can lead them to interact with these children differently than their middle-class peers. For example, the feedback that teachers provide to children they perceive as academically capable is typically content-related, whereas those children who are not perceived as capable receive feedback that is often control-related. Even the way teachers communicate praise is affected by their perceptions of students' academic abilities. The praise received by "highly capable" children tends to be more academic in nature than that received by "lower-ability" children (Rist, 1970). Not surprisingly, non-mainstream children can detect when a teacher does not expect much of them academically, and they often respond to this information in self-defeating ways, as will be demonstrated below (see Miller, 1995, for an overview of the literature on teacher expectation effects).

Non-Mainstream Students' Responses to Low Teacher Expectations and Cultural Incongruity in the Classroom

I now wish to cite three broad types of reactions that non-mainstream students can exhibit when they perceive that teachers have low estimations of their abilities. These three types of reactions are only intended as discrete illustrations; they are not intended to systematically represent the great variety of attitudes and behaviors that characterize educationally disadvantaged students. One way that certain students respond to teachers who have low academic expectations for them is to find non-academic roles in classroom life in which they can please their teachers. Black girls, for instance, tend to employ this strategy. In Linda Grant's (1984) case studies of six elementary school classrooms, she observed that while both black and white girls receive less academic feedback in heterogeneous classrooms than do black and white boys (black boys receive primarily negative feedback), black girls receive especially little. However, they are praised extensively for their social skills. The black girls that Grant observed demonstrated a "precocious social maturity." For instance, they often functioned in classrooms as "social care-takers" or "go-betweens," helping to maintain relational and communication links between teachers and students and between different groups of students (p. 106). Yet by adopting this social care-taker orientation in the classroom as opposed to a more academic posture, black females potentially limit their own future opportunities for economic independence and mobility. Moreover, the phenomenon described above is not limited to black girls. White girls are also commonly perceived as social care-takers. However, for white girls, their teachers often have high academic expectations of them at the same time they expect them to perform certain social roles in the classroom. The assignment of black girls to social care-taker roles is often less ambivalent (Grant, 1984).

Another way that non-mainstream students react to their struggles in school is to simply "cool out." This casual term does have origins in the educational research literature, but I am taking some liberties with it and some information on its original usage is helpful. Following Burton Clark (1960), Jerome Karabel (1972) uses the term to describe how disadvantaged students at junior colleges are often persuaded—through "realistic" counsel based on their academic performance—that higher education is not for them. Although I am both reversing the agency associated with the term and applying it to a younger population, I think that "cooling out" is an accurate description of what takes place in the minds of many non-mainstream students during their first several years in school. After a few years of unsuccessfully trying to compete with their middle-class peers, many non-mainstream students accept the verdict that they are academically mediocre at best. They resign themselves to going through the motions in school, and their academic performance deteriorates as a result.

The two types of reactions reviewed above are similar in that neither reaction is incompatible with a continued trust on the part of non-mainstream students that the educational system they inhabit is fair. Non-mainstream students can redefine their classroom roles or silently surrender their academic ambitions without necessarily concluding that the educational system has failed them. This is not always the case, however. Many non-mainstream students do conclude that the schools are failing them, rather than vice versa. These students take note that the subjects they study, and the ways in which they study these subjects, are often culturally foreign to them. Or, these students observe that no matter how hard they try, they cannot communicate their intelligence to their teachers. Perceiving their marginal positions in middle-class classrooms, non-mainstream children often choose to direct their minds and talents toward interactions that offer them more positive feedback. They develop amongst themselves a peer network that finds its identity in resisting their teachers, as opposed to pleasing them. The techniques of resistance often are very subtle. Non-mainstream children learn to appear compliant in the classroom, while at the same time communicating hidden messages to one another that convey their contempt for their teachers (Erickson, 1987). For these children, academic failure begins to be seen as an achievement, a sign that they have not sold themselves to the futile agenda their "hosts" have set for them (McDermott, 1987).

In all of the processes described above, teachers' low expectations of their non-mainstream students function as self-fulfilling prophecies. Social-psychologist Robert Merton invented the phrase "self-fulfilling prophecy" in 1957 to describe our human tendency to fulfill others' expectations of us, regardless of whether we are capable of accomplishing more or less than these expectations. In 1968, Robert Rosenthal and Lenore Jacobson applied Merton's theory to elementary school classrooms. In their now infamous experiment, Rosenthal and Jacobson falsely told a group of teachers that certain children in their classrooms had shown evidence, based on a "respected test," that they would "spurt" academically that year. They claim that this information heightened the teachers' expectations of the "spurters," and as a result, these spurters did achieve larger academic gains than other students. The research methods Rosenthal and Jacobson employed have been widely criticized, but few have questioned the rather common sense assumption that students respond to their teachers' expectations of them. The theory of the self-fulfilling prophecy is helpful because it captures the way in which non-mainstream students' reactions to their struggles in school—perfectly rational reactions—ultimately lead them to adopt attitudes and behaviors which reinforce their teachers' low expectations of them. Since low expectations contribute to the academic struggles of non-mainstream students in the first place, a vicious cycle ensues.

Ability Grouping and Tracking Practices as a Source of Educational Disadvantagement

The processes described thus far have been fairly implicit, focusing on the complex, cumulative interactions through which teachers often form and communicate lower expectations for non-mainstream students, and how students pick up on these low expectations and actually fulfill them through a variety of self-defeating behaviors. At this point, it is important to examine an explicit, mediating practice through which differential teacher expectations translate into differential treatment of non-mainstream students: the practice of ability-grouping at the elementary school level, or curricular tracking at the secondary level. This discussion is central to the conflict theorists' thesis because teachers' perceptions of children's cognitive ability have been shown to be a stronger predictor of ability-group placement than actual quantitative measures such as test scores or prior grades (Bennett & LeCompte, 1990, as cited in Knapp and Woolverton, 1995). If teachers' perceptions of non-mainstream students' abilities are unduly influenced by cultural factors, then their ability-grouping decisions are unfounded. Indeed, several conflict-oriented theorists have made this very assertion. For instance, Ray Rist's (1970) ethnographic study of several all-black elementary schools in St. Louis suggested that teachers' initial ability-group assignments were influenced by attributes of appearance like skin pigmentation, hair characteristics, and dress style, and that these attributes corresponded with traditional measures of socio-economic status such as welfare and single-parent status. B. Machler (1969) observed that teachers' initial ability-group assignments were heavily influenced by social skills such as politeness and willingness to follow directions that are clearly unrelated to students' cognitive abilities (cited in Hurn, 1993).

However, subsequent quantitative studies have repeatedly failed to demonstrate that children's socio-economic or racial status significantly impacts teachers' ability-group placement decisions at the elementary level, independent of cognitive ability (Haller & Davis, 1980; Haller, 1985; Sorensen & Hallinan, 1984; Gamoran, 1989). Given this fact, the conclusions of Rist's and Machler's particular observational studies cannot be generalized. These quantitative findings are damaging to an uncompromising conflict theory which asserts that non-mainstream children arrive at school with adequate intellectual development, and that their disproportionate placement in low-ability groups is a direct manifestation of ethno-centric discrimination on the part of their teachers. A more moderate conflict theory, however, does not necessarily rely upon proof of cultural favoritism. According to this moderate conflict perspective, the fact that ability-group placement decisions in primary school are relatively free of direct social-class bias does not mean that these decisions are morally justifiable. If ability-grouping practices result in inferior learning experiences for lower-ability students, which will be demonstrated below, then this practice cannot be justified until it can be said with confidence that students have spent a sufficient number of years in school to demonstrate their native learning potential independent of family and neighborhood influences. This is a very complex empirical question to which there is no clear answer, but I would argue that elementary-age students, particularly those in the primary grades, have not been in school nearly long enough for educators to have teased out native ability from mere cultural advantage or disadvantage deriving from students' home environments. Since there is very little mobility across ability groups throughout the elementary school years (Rist, 1970; Machler, 1969; Eder, 1981), and a strong correlation exists between membership in low ability groups in elementary school and low-track status in secondary school (Rosenbaum, 1976; Oakes, 1985; Hallinan & Sorensen, 1985), the impact of initial ability-group placement decisions upon children's futures are profound and often permanent.

The reason why the assignment of non-mainstream students to low-abi ity-groups in disproportionate numbers is problematic is that the quality of instruction is inferior in these groups. While it might seem like grouping low students together would enhance instructional time because a teacher can gear her teaching more specifically to the ability level of students, there is much evidence to the contrary. Two comparative studies of high and low-ability reading groups illustrate this point. Donna Eder (1981) studied the consequences of ability grouping in Wisconsin kindergarten classrooms, and McDermott (1977) studied the same phenomenon in New York City elementary schools. In all of the classrooms studied, children developed their reading skills by taking turns reading aloud to their group. Both studies concluded that low-ability students received much less time reading aloud than those in high-ability groups, essentially due to management problems caused by disruptive and inattentive students. Neither scholar blamed the teachers, but rather concluded that the practice of grouping young children by perceived academic ability—perceptions which, at this stage, are highly influenced by class-related, behavioral characteristics of students—creates small group cultures that serve the students within them in very unequal ways. Clearly, reading instruction is only one aspect of an academic program, and we have not addressed the effects of ability grouping in mathematics, which is also common. But success in reading is clearly foundational for students' academic futures, and these observational studies strongly suggest that low-ability children are educationally under-served anytime they are all grouped together and isolated from their more fortunate peers. In this case, recent quantitative research has begun to corroborate the ethnographers' findings. Adam Gamoran (1986), for example, found that the pace of reading differed sharply between high and low-ability reading groups, and that this pace difference served to widen the gap between strong and weak students' reading achievement throughout the school year.

Again, the cumulative reading achievement differences between non-mainstream and mainstream students are just one aspect of more general ability-grouping effects that include mathematics as well. Fully apart from the effects of ability grouping on elementary students' self-esteem, peer relationships, and democratic sentiments, the balance of quantitative research demonstrates that academic achievement differences widen from the time of students' initial group placements throughout their school careers (Alexander, Cook, & McDill, 1978; Alexander & McDill, 1976; Gamoran, 1987, Heyns, 1974; see Alexander & Cook, 1982; Jencks & Brown, 1975, for contradictory findings). Consequently, if non-mainstream students disproportionately occupy lower ability groups throughout their school careers, significant differences between these students and their mainstream counterparts are not surprising. Now, the functionalists' claim, based on status attainment research, that high schools do not directly discriminate against non-mainstream students, but merely reward cognitive ability, might be sustainable (see Kariger, 1962; Cicourel & Kitsuse, 1963; Oakes, 1985; Oakes, Gamoran, & Page, 1992, for less optimistic perspectives). There is also much evidence that social class has only a small effect on secondary school track placements, independent of prior measures of student ability (see Gamoran, 1989; Hurn, 1993). Indeed, it appears that black students—one of the primary subjects of concern in the cultural difference agenda— actually benefit from inappropriate placements. For example, Gamoran demonstrates that when black sophomores match non-black sophomores on achievement test scores and other social background attributes, blacks actually "enjoy substantially higher likelihood of placement in the college track than their white counterparts" (1989, pp. 1165-1166). Still, the thesis advanced here is that even if secondary schools are meritocratic places, and even if primary school ability-group placements are based on cognitive ability more than cultural factors—all of which is at least debatable—low-ability students should not be separated from their peers in their earliest years of school. Since non-mainstream students occupy low-ability groups in disproportionate numbers, their educational futures are harmed by primary schooling practices which exacerbate non-school related inequalities that are entirely beyond their control.

V. A Dissenting Opinion:
The Possible Influence of I.Q.
in Determining
Unequal Educational Achievement

A Review of Herrnstein and Murray's
Arguments As Presented in The Bell Curve *(1994)*

Although ability-grouping practices at the elementary school level were critiqued above, the interactionist perspective is generally careful to avoid holding either non-mainstream students or their schools solely responsible for their educational under-performance. However, throughout the last three decades of debate about the causes of educational disadvantagement, a minority view has asserted that inter-group differences in achievement are partly a result of genetically-determined differences in average intelligence, differences which are not the schools' fault and are highly resistant to educational intervention (Jensen, 1969, 1973, 1985; Herrnstein, 1971, 1973). Since the major recommendation of this book is that we need to take the role of educational institutions in equalizing opportunities more seriously than we have in recent years, and that one measure of success is increasing parity across ethnic groups in academic and occupational achievement, this highly controversial argument must be adequately addressed if this project is to be persuasive. The topic cannot be avoided; as recently as 1994, Richard J. Herrnstein and Charles Murray re-articulated Jensen's and Herrnstein's previous argument in the best-selling book, *The Bell Curve*. I turn now to an analysis of their arguments.

Herrnstein and Murray identify two groups of people that occupy the extreme ends of a bell curve distribution based on what is commonly described as a person's I.Q., or intelligence quotient: a "cognitive elite" and a "cognitive underclass." While Herrnstein and Murray do refer to Asian-Americans in their analysis, their discussion focuses on differences between Caucasians and African-Americans, who are disproportionately represented in the elite and underclass groups respectively. When measured as a group, not as individuals—a clarification that cannot be over-emphasized—whites outscore blacks on I.Q. tests by about fifteen points; this is statistically significant and is not contestable. What has been contested is Herrnstein and Murray's claim that the differences in "intelligence" that separate whites and blacks—to the degree that such a phenomenon exists—arise from natural and genetic, as well as social and environmental sources. While Herrnstein and Murray's argument for genetic cognitive inequality is "taboo," as they put it, in public, many thinkers do struggle with this question in private. Indeed, in the introduction to *A Piece of the Pie: Blacks and White Immigrants Since 1880*—Stanley Lieberson's historical comparison of educational and occupational opportunities for blacks and whites in America—Lieberson acknowledges that it was the painful dissonance between his public pronouncements and his private suspicions that prompted him to explore the question in the first place (1980, p. xi).

Herrnstein and Murray's main objective is to demonstrate that intelligence—as measured by I.Q. scores—predicts peoples' social performance—high school and college completion, gainful employment, economic stability, and marital and parental success—more accurately than does socio-economic status, and that attempts at egalitarian social change based on improving poor persons' cultural capital are likely to disappoint. Consequently, Herrnstein and Murray believe that educational reform, as the reigning strategy for improving the life chances of disadvantaged children, is of dubious value. In order to make this point, Herrnstein and Murray recall the findings of the Coleman Report in the mid-1960s, the largest social science survey of its time, which concluded that "variations in teacher credentials, per pupil expenditures, and other objective factors in public schools do not account for much of the variation in cognitive abilities of American school children" (quoted in Herrnstein & Murray, p. 395). The authors also argue that while compensatory programs for disadvantaged students, such as Head Start, produce short-term cognitive gains, these gains fade over time. "As of now," they conclude, "the goal of raising intelligence among school-age children more than modestly, and doing so consistently remains out of reach" (p. 402). Furthermore, Herrnstein and Murray argue that the one real effect of the 1960s and 1970s efforts at educational equalization was that gifted children were underserved. Relying upon data from Scholastic Aptitude Tests (SAT) administered between 1963 and 1980, the authors point to "a downward trend of the educational skills of America's most academically promising youngsters toward those of the average student" (p. 427), and they draw the following conclusion: "One of the chief effects of the educational reforms of the 1960s was to dumb down elementary and secondary education as a whole, making just about everything easier for the average student and easing the demands on the gifted student" (p. 430).

In terms of specific policy recommendations, Herrnstein and Murray's advocacy of the educational excellence perspective over the equal opportunity perspective is not surprising.[1] They urge liberal reformers "to come to terms with the reality that in a universal education system, many students will not reach the level of education that most people view as basic" (p. 436). Given this fact, policy-makers should "reallocate some portion of existing elementary and secondary school federal aid away from programs for the disadvantaged to programs for the gifted" (p. 441). Alongside their recommendation that educators surrender their "high hopes" and "flamboyant claims" about the prospects of raising the intelligence level of the cognitive underclass, Herrnstein and Murray include a curious pitch for publicly funded private school choice, with no explicit rationale provided. I suspect that the authors' view is that the children of the cognitive elite, who are most likely intellectually well-endowed themselves, should have the opportunity to attend schools with equally well-endowed peers, and that this would occur by self-selection if a school choice plan were in place. To be fair, it should be noted that exceptionally bright children from the lower classes would be welcome at the selective schools; cognitive segregation does not necessarily entail complete socio-economic segregation, although if one accepts Herrnstein and Murray's hypothesis it might come close.

A Response to Herrnstein and Murray's Arguments

This topic is both highly complex and highly sensitive, so I must respond carefully and modestly. As for Herrnstein and Murray's argument for meritocracy—that intelligence as measured by I.Q. scores is the strongest predictor of individuals' educational and occupational success—this claim fails for the same reason that the status attainment research reviewed above fails. Regarding this claim, the sole data on intelligence that the authors rely upon is taken from the National Longitudinal Survey of Labor Market Experience of Youth (NLSY) project that began in 1979, which administered four sub-sections of the Armed Forces Qualification Test (AFQT) to 12,000 youth between the ages of 14 and 22 and representing a variety of socio-economic classes and ethnic groups. The four sub-sections utilized tested word knowledge, paragraph comprehension, arithmetic reasoning, and general mathematical knowledge, and significant differences between socio-economic and ethnic groups did occur. Like the status-attainment research reviewed above, Herrnstein and Murray's claim that these measures of cognitive ability exert a stronger independent effect on social outcomes than either socio-economic status or race is valid. This should give pause to strict conflict-oriented theorists who adamantly assert that direct race-based or class-based discrimination is the best explanation of unequal occupational outcomes across social groups. However, also like the status-attainment research, this finding does not strongly aid the meritocratic thesis. The problem with this argument is that what Herrnstein and Murray are calling I.Q. is more accurately described as an indicator of academic learning, or knowledge, and does not account for differing educational experiences across social groups that occurred between birth and adolescence. If educational opportunities for the children of our society are widely disparate across social classes and ethnic groups, then the claim that discrimination does not unduly effect the chances of persons in their teens and twenties is not sufficient to support an argument for meritocracy.

If intelligence is not the same thing as academic learning or knowledge, then what is it, assuming that it is in some way identifiable? Although many might question any reliance on Arthur Jensen (1969, 1973, 1985), Herrnstein's predecessor and one of the most influential of the recent hereditarians, I think he has given a solid, if basic answer to this question. Jensen describes intelligence in terms of cognitive processing skills, such as the ability to deal with abstractions and to form concepts and ideas (1985). While acknowledging that these cognitive skills represent a mere slice of the attributes of a talented person, they are the skills that have helped develop modern industrial societies, and which such societies reward in individuals. They are also, he asserts, the skills that schools are supposed to develop, and which both I.Q. tests and academic achievement tests reflect in quantitative terms (1985). Now, in his recent book, *Multiple Intelligences* (1993), Howard Gardner persuasively argues that the cognitive processing skills which schools teach and I.Q. tests reward are unnecessarily restricted to linguistic and mathematical processes, and do not address the many other human talents—such as music, athletics, or interpersonal communication—that are also reflective of cognitive processing abilities, although perhaps more subtly. However, linguistic and quantitative talents are disproportionately rewarded in our society, and the recommendation of this book is that we enhance educational and occupational opportunities for non-mainstream children, rather than completely re-conceptualize the logic of our existing distributive system. Thus, I believe that defining intelligence as linguistic and quantitative cognitive processing abilities—and gearing assessment measures to these processes—is a sufficient improvement over Herrnstein and Murray's implicit reliance on absolute measures of young persons' academic knowledge. Perhaps the boundaries between the former and the latter definitions of intelligence are quite fluid, but the distinction is important nonetheless.

Although Jensen's arguments concerning intelligence, intelligence testing, and schooling have been challenged by others at every turn (see Jacoby & Glauberman, 1995; Fraser, 1995, for collections of critiques), I agree with him on certain points. I can accept his description of intelligence as the generic ability to think abstractly, to grasp new ideas, and to process complex information. I can tentatively accept his belief that this human capacity is distinguishable and roughly measurable. I can also tentatively accept his assertion that recent tests designed to measure intelligence are increasingly free of cultural bias, given the evidence that blacks and whites miss the same items, rather than there being some items which all whites know and many blacks do not for reasons of cultural unfamiliarity (1969). On average, blacks and whites do score significantly different on these tests. Despite their erroneous decision to use NLSY scores as a proxy for intelligence, Herrnstein and Murray also share all of these convictions, including the more controversial one that I do not share about the strength of genetic factors in explaining blacks' inferior scores on intelligence tests. Actually, Herrnstein and Murray do not "come clean" on the question of the relative power of genetic versus environmental factors in determining intelligence. Unlike Jensen, who ventured a guess that heredity accounts for eighty percent of an individual's intellectual capacity, Herrnstein and Murray claim to be "agnostic" about the question (p. 311). However, their analysis and recommendations concerning federal compensatory education efforts, as described above, betray this disclaimer. They seem to think that the ambiguous results of one decade of compensatory education efforts provide conclusive evidence that the intellectual capacity of a disproportionately black underclass of children is highly resistant to environmental and educational intervention. I do not think such a conclusion is warranted.

Ironically, the founders of compensatory education in the 1960s had the same faulty, knowledge-centered conception of intelligence that Herrnstein and Murray demonstrate by their assumption that the linguistic, reading, and mathematics sections of the AFQT actually capture the native intelligence of 14-22 year-olds. Reflecting back on the beginning of the compensatory movement which he partly founded, Edward Zigler describes how 1960s-era liberal reformers naively assumed that basic pull-out programs (Chapter One) and pre-school programs (Head Start) would easily bring disadvantaged children up to the cognitive level of their more advantaged peers. It was assumed that these compensatory programs did not need to teach in a qualitatively different manner, but merely needed to provide more time for disadvantaged children to gain basic academic skills and acquire necessary bits of knowledge. In Zigler and Berman's words: "What we witnessed in the 1960s was the belief that intelligence quotients can be dramatically increased with minimal effort.... Unfortunately, 'knowing more' was easily translated [in their thinking] into 'becoming smarter' " (1983, p. 895). And Zigler means "minimal effort": "We actually thought

we could compensate for the effects of several years of impoverishment as well as inoculate the child against the future ravages
of such impoverishment, all by providing a six or eight-week
summer Head Start experience" (quoted in Skerry, 1983). As
Zigler now knows, a multi-year—even multi-generational—
commitment to continuous compensatory assistance to disadvantaged children, complemented by a whole set of broader
social reforms of which educational efforts are just one part,
would be necessary to dent the learning deficit of a disproportionately black underclass. Most importantly, the education-
related aspect of this reform would benefit from recent research
into cognitive processing and critical thinking, such that the
explicit aim of new educational efforts would be to improve
thinking skills and not to simply convey information. This is not
to mention adjustments to regular classroom instructional delivery that often works against non-mainstream children, as reviewed in the prior section. In the final chapter, I will cite some
current compensatory efforts that are indeed having a positive
impact on children's cognitive-processing abilities, which I believe to be a satisfactory conception of—or at least a reasonable
proxy for—intelligence.

It is important to acknowledge that Jensen's estimation that
any given individual's intelligence is eighty percent determined
by genetic factors has been discounted by most experts in recent
years, but they have not denied genetic influence by any means.
After a review of the recent research, Robert Plomin (1989)
estimates that the relative effects of genes and environment are
about equal. After surveying over one thousand experts in the
field, Snyderman and Rothman (1987) report that the average of
these experts' estimates of the influence of hereditary factors is
about sixty percent. If environmental influences account for
roughly one-half of any given individual's intelligence—assuming that existing measures are actually getting at it—then we
cannot assume that any individual's educational and occupa-

tional performance is a simple reflection of the opportunities she has been given. However, a 40 to 50 percent degree of environmental influence is easily large enough to explain group differences between blacks and whites—which are determined by simply aggregating individual scores—given the obvious fact that most blacks were denied mainstream educational opportunities until very recently, and blacks are still disproportionately represented among today's urban underclass. In a groundbreaking piece of historiography, Thomas Sowell (1977) has shown that almost all of the southern and eastern European ethnic groups that immigrated to America earlier this century lagged behind white natives in I.Q. scores until they assimilated into the dominant culture. For a whole set of complex reasons related to race, blacks are assimilating much more slowly, and so the gap will close more slowly. And, even Herrnstein and Murray admit that the gap is currently diminishing (p. 292). As Hurn (1993) stated upon reviewing the history concerning white and non-white differences on measures of I.Q., black-white differences "are in no way unique and do not require any special explanation" (p. 149). My apologies to readers who were pained by the explanation just provided, but it was necessary to deal with the bell curve thesis if I am recommending proportional representation in desirable occupations across ethnic groups as a worthy measure of the degree to which substantive equality of opportunity exists in American society.

VI. A Brief Portrait
of An Educationally Disadvantaged
Young Man

The Case of Ronald Grady

Before concluding the chapter, I wish to respond personally to the discussion of educational disadvantagement above by creating a composite character drawn from my own memories about two young men I taught in the Rainier Valley area of Seattle, Washington. I will first recount some memories of "Ronald Grady," and then reflect on my experience with him in light of some of the ideas and concepts presented in this chapter. Ronald Grady is a lanky fifteen-year-old with a keen intelligence and an infectious grin. He is a handsome young man, imposing even, and a leader among his friends. However, Ronald possesses several background characteristics that make him a likely candidate to struggle in school. In addition to being black, Ronald no longer has contact with his father, who left the family when Ronald was quite young. Ronald lives with his mother, his grandmother, and two older sisters. His older brother is in prison. Although Ronald's mother works two jobs, the family struggles to make ends meet. Ronald's mother has little time to help him with homework. However, even if she did have time to help Ronald, she might not be the most effective tutor because she is not highly educated herself.

Ronald spends almost all his non-school time cruising the back streets of South Seattle. His favorite haunts are under-supervised arcade centers, bowling alleys, and rental houses occupied by street kids just barely older than himself. Ronald can be described as a gang-leader in training, learning each day to more effectively bully his peers, to steal whatever he desires, and to elude authorities. As for his schooling experiences, several years ago Ronald was assigned to a program for "at risk" middle-school children in which I was the main teacher. On those days when Ronald actually came to class, he usually made things interesting. He was an amazingly gifted consumer of stories—not as a reader but as a listener or viewer—both in terms of factual details and larger themes. I had to make a conscious effort not to allow class discussions to turn into one-on-one debates between myself and Ronald. But as for other subjects like math, science, or grammar—at least the way I taught them—I rarely was able to engage Ronald. This was Ronald's fault as much as my own. For instance, Ronald had very little patience when he was confused. He had interpreted his past schooling experiences as evidence that he was "dumb," and he often was too tired for school work after his nights of carousing.

Given the recent phenomenon of educational inflation, which entails that a certain level of education buys less than it used to in the job market (Milner, 1972), the prospects for Ronald look dim. Even if he completes high school, which is doubtful, it is unlikely that he will attend college and escape a working-class future. Actually, such an outcome might be the best that can be hoped for; the number of black young men jailed or killed as a result of gang-involvement is shocking, and unemployment or welfare are also strong possibilities. If any of these tragic outcomes does in fact occur, it will be a case of wasted potential. Like any healthy child, Ronald grew up with big dreams. But by the time I knew him he was already realizing that his dreams might not come true. In addition to his gift for stories, Ronald has the honesty of a poet. Here is a poem he wrote—based on a simple rhythmic formula that I had taught him—that painfully chronicles the death of his dreams:

I used to play football
Now I play streetfighter
I used to have unmarked skin
Now I have tatoos
I used to like the color purple
Now I love black
I used to be a good kid
Now I'm a gang banger
I used to be addicted to school
Now I'm addicted to money
I used to have dreams and hopes
Now I have money and cocaine
I used to be alive
Now I am dead

Questions about Ronald's Schooling Experience

Reflecting back on my experience as Ronald's middle-school teacher, I might take comfort in the functionalist explanation of educational disadvantagement, which effectively resolves me of partial responsibility for Ronald's academic struggles. At the time I knew him, Ronald's scores on standardized measures of cognitive ability were quite low, as were his course grades over the last few years. While I am sure that I have many blind spots concerning my interactions with non-mainstream students, I know that I tried to assess his performance as fairly as possible, and I think the other teacher who worked with Ronald did the same. On this basis, I might conclude that it was Ronald's cognitive ability and academic performance that determined his fate, more than some complex process of discrimination that penalized him for his low socio-economic or racial-minority status. Thus, the school at which I worked might still claim to be meritocratic, or at least I could think so.

I am haunted, however, by some of the issues raised in this

chapter about non-mainstream children's experiences in primary school. I might already have a few answers to these questions if I had researched Ronald's elementary records more thoroughly than I did, but the questions still plague me: How adept were Ronald's primary school teachers at disentangling his native intellectual potential from the effects of social-class related contingencies such as an absent father and a mother who by necessity had to work when more fortunate mothers were home with their children? Did Ronald's African-American cultural identity manifest itself in any ways that were legitimate, but which estranged him from those teachers who were white? In other words, were the expectations his teachers formed about him reasonably free of cultural bias? Also, did Ronald's primary school educators utilize ability-grouping practices before non-mainstream students had sufficient time to respond positively to learning opportunities in the classroom? If the answers to any of these questions would fulfill the negative suspicions of conflict theorists, what were the effects on Ronald? When he told me he was "dumb," was this evidence that he had internalized the judgement of our school system delivered to him over the past eight years? Was this why he vacillated between open hostility to our school and my classroom and a more passive resignation concerning his place as an "alternative" student?

I do not know the answers to these questions about Ronald's experience in South Seattle elementary schools, but I think they are the right questions to be asking about the American school system in general. Finally, I do not intend my reflections on Ronald's experience to be misunderstood as implying that secondary schools treat non-mainstream students more fairly than elementary schools do, or worse yet, that I treated Ronald more fairly than his primary-level teachers did. The vast majority of elementary teachers deal with non-mainstream students in the best way they know how. If it is true that the academic problems of educationally disadvantaged students can often be traced to highly impactful schooling practices that they encountered in their first years of school, then it might simply be concluded that elementary education is more critical in terms of equity issues than secondary institutions. Hence, our research and reform efforts should focus there, as much of the recent ethnographic research has done. As a secondary teacher I might resist this possibility, but the evidence presented in this chapter is persuasive.

VII. Conclusion: Educational Disadvantagement and Inequality of Educational Opportunity

In the preceding discussion, I have presented a moderate version of the conflict theorists' explanation of educational disadvantagement, or the disproportionate failure rates of non-mainstream students. I have presented a culture-centered interactionist perspective, which asserts that lower-class families do not always sufficiently prepare their children for schooling, but also acknowledges that middle-class educators often evaluate students in an ethno-centric manner that works to the disadvantage of non-mainstream students. I have critiqued the practice of ability grouping in elementary schools in particular, arguing that it is inappropriate to separate students by ability at this age because they have not spent nearly enough time in schools for their teachers to distinguish between native cognitive capacity and the effects of educational inequalities arising from their home environments.

In concluding this chapter, I want to make the connection between educational disadvantagement and inequality of educational opportunity as explicit as possible. If it is true that primary-school teachers are making ability-grouping assignments years before they have truly disentangled ability from mere cultural advantage or disadvantage—and we know that disproportionate numbers of non-mainstream students occupy the low-ability groups, and also that ability-group placements typically endure over children's elementary and even secondary careers—then non-mainstream children are being penalized, if only indirectly, for circumstances beyond their control. Given this picture, it becomes evident that inequality of educational results between different socio-economic and racial and ethnic groups is in large part a problem of inequality of educational opportunity. It is the latter charge, not the former, that motivates this project. In the chapter that follows, I turn to a philosophical defense of my vision of substantive equality of opportunity.

Note

1. See Chapter One for a review of these perspectives.

Chapter Three

Opportunities of Substance:
Revisiting Equality of Opportunity as a Moral Ideal

I. Chapter Preview

The guiding objective of this chapter is to present as clearly as possible the historical roots and the philosophical rationale for a substantive vision of equality of opportunity. I will begin the chapter by examining substantive equality of opportunity in detail, defining it as a liberal, meritocratic, and prospect-regarding ideal, although I have not yet introduced this last term. I will then support my conception of substantive equality of opportunity by appealing to certain elements of the historic liberal tradition in political philosophy, specifically the assumptions regarding the moral equality of persons that informed early liberal thinkers, and also the transition from a negative to a positive conception of liberty as presented in the revised liberalism of the last few decades (Smith, 1968, p. 281). Finally, I will review the major criticisms of meritocratic equality of opportunity that have been articulated in recent years, and then assess the impact of these criticisms on the thesis advanced in this project.

II. Substantive Equality of Opportunity as Defined So Far

Substantive Equality of Opportunity as a Liberal Ideal

At this point in the project, I have not yet attempted to explicitly separate the concept of equality of educational opportunity from its parent concept of general equality of opportunity. I will address equality of educational opportunity specifically in the next chapter, but the present discussion will reveal that its relationship with the general ideal is quite fluid. My vision of substantive equality of opportunity can be described as liberal, meritocratic, and prospect-regarding, characteristics which I will now discuss in turn. As a liberal ideal, substantive equality of opportunity is understood to be a right possessed by individual persons, a right to similar life chances, or similar prospects for occupational and economic success. As the Latin root of the term "liberal" implies,[1] liberal theories are fundamentally concerned with individual liberty, and substantive equality of opportunity possesses moral importance because occupational opportunity is understood to be an essential element of individual liberty. However, as stated in Chapter One, there is also an equality assumption in liberalism. All persons, by virtue of being human, possess equal rights to personal liberty and occupational opportunity, and no individual can exploit opportunities in a manner that impedes the right of another person to do the same.

I am aware of the risks involved in presenting my vision of substantive equality of opportunity under the liberal label. As the dominant paradigm for Western political philosophy, liberalism is always under attack by alternative paradigms such as libertarianism (see, i.e., Nozick, 1974), communitarianism (see, i.e., Taylor, 1979; Sandel, 1982), and critical theory (see, i.e., Habermas, 1975; Freire, 1970). I am not sympathetic to the libertarian agenda, at least not Nozick's brand. While I am more sympathetic to the motivating sentiments behind communitarianism, I do not agree with those who see liberalism as logically incompatible with these sentiments, but will not elaborate on this point because it is not directly relevant to my concern with distributive justice. However, I would regret it if someone loyal to the critical paradigm too quickly dismissed my project because it appeared to be anchored in "status-quo" liberal theory. Before I explain why this is so, I must define critical theory briefly.

The family of social and political theories that make up the critical paradigm is diverse in purpose and form, but one very general characteristic that marks these theories as critical is identifiable. Critical theories, whether they address epistemological, socio-structural, or specific policy concerns, seek to promote social justice by uncovering any elements of the ideological "status-quo" that allow one group of persons in a society to maintain control over the political and economic affairs of others. Regarding my specific concern with distributive issues, critical theorists often have noted that the classical liberal commitment to unbridled economic liberty for all individuals is ultimately self-defeating. I would agree, and merely add that modern liberals such as Kenneth Strike and John Rawls—whose views will be discussed in detail below—understand this as well. Readers who are loyal to the critical paradigm can form their own judgements, but I would submit that there is no crucial difference between the critical model of distributive equity and the revised liberal model presented as the chapter unfolds.

Substantive Equality of Opportunity as a Meritocratic Ideal

Substantive equality of opportunity can also be described as a meritocratic ideal. Indeed, the idea of social rewards being determined by one's performance, or merit, is what most people think of when they hear the term "equal opportunity." In Chapter One, I introduced the important distinction between the formal and substantive interpretations of equal opportunity, and I now wish to draw a parallel distinction concerning the concept of meritocracy. One might describe the formal understanding of meritocracy as present-oriented and the substantive understanding as developmentally-oriented. Under the formal, present-oriented model, the race for scarce occupational and economic rewards begins in elementary school—where the process of differentiating between talented and untalented persons first takes form—and continues unceasingly throughout these persons' lives. The goal in a formal meritocracy, from primary school on up, is always to be fair in the present moment, judging each child's capacity for certain opportunities—such as enrollment in gifted programs or inclusion in high-ability groups within individual classrooms—by relevant and objective criteria such as classroom and standardized test performance. However, while the emphasis on evaluation and promotion procedures that are fair in the moment is admirable, it fails to adequately recognize two crucial problems.

First, the formal understanding of meritocracy fails to recognize that student placement decisions in elementary and secondary schools—even those that are based on as objective criteria as possible—are often inappropriate because there has not been sufficient time to accurately tease out native talent from mere cultural advantage. As demonstrated in the previous chapter, children who come from home situations that are educationally mainstream or affluent arrive at elementary school a "leg up" on their peers, regardless of whether or not they truly possess superior native ability. This inequality between mainstream and non-mainstream social groups regarding what educators call school readiness is not a shocking problem in itself; Americans always have assumed that different social classes possess differing abilities to prepare their children for school. However, Americans also have hoped—following Thomas Jefferson, Horace Mann, and Lyndon Johnson, whose views will be discussed in the next chapter—that public schooling is powerful enough to counter-balance educational inequalities that arise from non-school sources, and that a few years in school is sufficient time for a child's true native ability to appear. Unfortunately, the balance of empirical evidence concerning the relative power of schooling to mitigate non-school educational inequalities does not support the traditional, sanguine assumption. If a few, or even several years in school are not sufficient time to allow each child's native ability to develop independent of social background variables, then the moral strength behind present-oriented, formally meritocratic school treatment decisions is seriously undermined.

Second, the formal understanding of meritocracy fails to recognize the inter-dependence between the successive opportunities that persons encounter throughout their lives. Opportunities build upon one another; a child who is placed in high-ability groups in elementary school is better prepared to compete for the academic track that awaits her in secondary school, and is then, in turn, better prepared to compete for admission to selective colleges, which gives her an advantage in the job market. Now, if the first few placement decisions in children's lives are in fact affected significantly by social background characteristics beyond their control, and if subsequent opportunities available to different children depend upon previous outcomes, then the whole system of opportunities is less than meritocratic. It is meritocratic in its discrete parts, but is not authentically meritocratic on the whole. This problem increases in significance as the years pass because the gap between persons on different tracks widens over time. For example, while opportunities such as admission to selective colleges might appear in the present to be based on criteria that "obviously" reflect true, native superiority, in many cases such superiority never existed—what appears as native superiority is merely the product of cultural advantages that have built upon one another over the first eighteen years of children's lives.

In a well-known essay on equality of opportunity and meritocracy, Charles Frankel (1971) acknowledges the problems with formal, present-oriented meritocracy that are described above (see also O'Neill, 1977). Frankel proposes an "educational" conception of equality of opportunity that is meant to stand alongside, but not to replace a purely meritocratic conception (Frankel, p. 204). Frankel's educational conception is similar to what I am calling substantive, developmentally-oriented meritocracy; he understands that meritocratic competition cannot simply begin at birth and proceed in linear fashion throughout people's lives. Purely meritocratic equality of opportunity must be temporally proceeded by educational opportunity that is developmentally-oriented and not meritocratic. Society must provide each child with a substantial period of years to pursue learning in an institutional environment that does not label or channel her based on some judgement of merit, however objective such a judgement is in the present moment. Exactly how many years of truly common schooling—where rich and poor, mainstream and non-mainstream children learn in the same classrooms and in the same groups—would be required before we could truly say that each child's native ability has had time to make itself known, independent of social background characteristics she inherited from her parents? This is a complex empirical question, and its answer depends not only on certain "facts" of educational psychology, but also on how effective educators can become at working with heterogeneous, as opposed to homogeneous, student populations (Oakes, 1992; Wheelock, 1996). What is less complex is the fact that our society cannot claim to be an authentic meritocracy until we choose to provide some years of schooling that are not meritocratic, where all children are given the necessary time to train for "the race," not to begin the race in their kindergarten year.

While the call for de-tracking at the secondary level and eliminating rigid ability-grouping practices at the elementary level is critical for creating substantive meritocracy in schools, heterogeneous grouping is not sufficient in and of itself. Additional compensatory measures, such as Head Start, Chapter One, and Upward Bound programs for educationally disadvantaged children, are necessary to counter-act inequalities in school readiness associated with cultural identity and socioeconomic status. Yet, according to the formal conception of meritocracy, the expenses attached to such compensatory programs create a problem. According to the formalists, the state is responsible to expend equal amounts of resources for all children and to ensure that no child experiences discriminatory treatment based on irrelevant attributes such as non-mainstream or poverty status. The extra spending attached to compensatory programs for targeted populations goes beyond the criteria of equal access, and is actually seen by formalists as promoting unequal educational opportunity in the interests of rigidly egalitarian ends.

However, this problem is avoided under the substantive model. As articulated in the first chapter, one critical distinction between the substantive and formal interpretations of meritocracy involves the concept of educational opportunity. Where the formal interpretation identifies educational opportunity solely with formal schooling—at least for purposes of policy—the substantive interpretation understands educational opportunity in much broader terms, including informal educative experiences arising from family and neighborhood sources alongside formal schooling as variables comprising a child's set of educational opportunities (Strike, 1988, p. 158). Given this expansive understanding of what constitutes educational opportunity for children, advocates of the substantive model argue that it is the moral duty of society to finance programs that assist children who are born into less advantageous social situations.

Substantive Equality of Opportunity as a Prospect-Regarding Ideal

Finally, substantive equality of opportunity can be described as what Barry Gross calls a "prospect-regarding," as opposed to a "means-regarding" ideal (1987, p. 124). As stated in Chapter One, the substantive conception of equal opportunity is prospect-regarding because its measure of success concerns the occupational and economic prospects, or life chances, of persons. The formal conception is means-regarding, on the other hand, because it seeks only to equalize access to desirable occupations and is not concerned whether or not different social groups actually possess statistically equivalent odds of attaining these positions. The substantive, prospect-regarding conception is often characterized as promoting equal results, or social leveling, which is meant derogatorily by its opponents and denied vigorously by its advocates. That social leveling is taken by both sides to be an unequivocal negative says something about the climate and ideological limits of the egalitarian debate in American society, but it is a misleading description of the substantive view in any respect. The equal results view does indeed hold to parity of economic success across certain social groups—such as those defined by occupationally irrelevant criteria like race or gender—as the best measure of equality of opportunity, but it is not concerned with equality of results across individuals within these groups. It is not imagined that all persons should be occupationally and economically on a par, but merely that large-scale social groupings defined by occupationally irrelevant criteria should experience roughly similar prospects. The specific requirements of substantive equality of opportunity will arise again as the project proceeds, but one clarification is immediately necessary.

The fact that equality of economic results across social groups is identified as the primary measure by which we can assess our progress regarding substantive equal opportunity should not be taken to imply that such a result should be attained by continuous interference with the occupational market-place. In other words, the measure of success for the substantive model— proportional representation in desirable occupations across all groups defined by characteristics irrelevant to job performance— is not an end that justifies any means. My vision of substantive equality of opportunity is not directly manipulative, as are affirmative action programs applied at the occupational level, which I consider to be a necessary evil. An authentic commitment to substantive equality of opportunity would alleviate the need for affirmative action over time because disadvantaged populations would benefit from vigorous compensatory assistance from early childhood on up, and inappropriate separating mechanisms such as ability grouping in elementary schools would be replaced by a commitment to effective instruction in heterogeneous classrooms. However, to say that my vision of substantive equality of opportunity is not directly manipulative is not to say that it is not interventionist. A commitment to funding education so that it truly can counter-balance non-school inequalities—addressing such issues as class size problems in mainstream settings and extra compensatory programs for the unfortunate—would clearly require large taxation increases for middle and upper-class citizens. But an interventionist taxation program does not necessarily imply a manipulation of occupational outcomes; the emphasis will remain on equalizing opportunity—not equalizing outcomes—throughout.

III. The Classical Liberal Commitment to Negative Liberty and the Equal Moral Worth of Persons

An Introduction to the Concepts
of Negative and Positive Liberty

Now that I have described my vision of substantive equality of opportunity as a liberal, meritocratic, and prospect-regarding ideal, my objective in the following section is to support this vision by appealing to the historic liberal tradition in political philosophy. I have characterized liberal political theory as being fundamentally concerned with protecting the liberty of all persons. The ideal of equality of opportunity arises out of liberalism because educational and occupational opportunity is an essential expression of personal liberty. I also have made a point of distinguishing between the formal and the substantive interpretations of equality of opportunity throughout the book, and another way to further clarify the difference between the two ideals is through the philosophical concept of negative and positive liberty (see Kant, 1964; Berlin, 1969). The formal conception of equal opportunity promotes negative liberty because it is concerned with the absence of certain objectionable practices, in this case discriminatory educational and occupational selection procedures based upon irrelevant characteristics such as race or gender. The substantive conception of equal opportunity promotes positive liberty because it is concerned with the presence of certain qualities, in this case the positive empowerment of individuals from various social backgrounds to attain educational and occupational success.

The distinction between the formal, negative conception of liberty and the substantive, positive conception corresponds with another distinction: the difference between classical and contemporary liberalism (see O'Neill, 1977). While the conception of substantive equality opportunity advanced here is ultimately grounded in the positive understanding of liberty proclaimed by modern liberals, it is important to address some classical liberal thinkers who laid the groundwork for the contemporary revisionists. The main contribution of these classical liberal thinkers is their insight into the equal moral worth of persons, which led them to assert that all individuals deserved equal concern and respect. I turn now to an examination of the reasons these classical liberals gave for their presumption of human equality, and also to a review of the implications of their belief in human equality for the organization of society.

The Claim For Human Equality on the Basis of Shared Passions

Amy Gutmann has observed that the concept of equality is typically employed by political philosophers in one of two ways. Philosophers either speak of human equality in a descriptive fashion, arguing that human beings are observably equal in one or another important respect, or they speak of social equality in a prescriptive fashion, arguing that human beings deserve to be treated equally in some important respect (1980). When speaking in descriptive terms, philosophers seek to discover the empirical basis for the claim that all men are created equal. On what basis—according to which faculties—can it be concluded that all persons are of equal moral worth? Clearly, all persons do not possess exactly equivalent physical strength, moral fortitude, or anything else, nor would anyone want this to be the case.

But are there certain qualities in which human beings are roughly similar to one another—and collectively distinguishable from other species—and on which basis we might confer equal moral worth? When speaking in prescriptive terms, philosophers turn to questions of social and political organization and ask themselves the following question: If all human beings are of equal moral worth, how is this human equality best respected in political practice?

Regarding the descriptive problem specifically, Gutmann has identified two major strands of what she calls "equality assumptions" in the classical liberal tradition (1980, p. 18). One of the strands that Gutmann identifies holds that human beings are equally valuable by virtue of the fact that they share similar "passions" (p. 20). Obviously, all persons do not experience identical emotions or desires and do not share identical goals in life, but they do share certain basic inclinations. Ironically, the first Western philosopher to build a political theory around the assumption of equal passions across persons did not advocate a liberal state, but rather a totalitarian monarchy. In his classic work *Leviathan*, Thomas Hobbes argues that all men are driven by two basic inclinations: "a perpetual and restless desire for power" and a deep-seated fear of death (1962, p. 75). The first inclination entails that mankind will impose upon itself a perpetual state of war, and the second inclination ensures that no one can be secure and content in such a tumultuous state. Hobbes' deeply illiberal solution is that all citizens should freely surrender their freedom to a king—an omnipotent and hopefully benevolent "leviathan"—and by so doing they will rid themselves of the ceaseless warring between would-be kings among them.

Although Jeremy Bentham envisioned a state that looked very different from Hobbes' totalitarian monarchy, he, and James Mill after him, picked up on Hobbes' idea of equal passions among persons. Bentham, however, labels the ruling passions differently: "Nature has placed mankind under the governance of two sovereign masters, pain and pleasure. It is for them alone to point out what we ought to do, as well as to determine what we shall do. On the one hand the standard of right and wrong, on the other the chain of causes and effects, are fastened to their throne" (1843, Ch. 1, Sect. 1). It is important to note that neither Bentham nor Mill mean to portray human beings as mere Pavlovian creatures stuck in an instinctual stimulus-response pattern concerning pain and pleasure. Both men, and Hobbes as well (1962, p. 98), understood that human beings are unique among living species in that they possess rationality. Still, in their view, rationality serves only an instrumental, organizing function, as the tool that individuals employ in order to maximize their pleasures—typically satisfied by wealth, power, and security—in the present moment and over the course of their whole lives. Bentham explains his view in this way: "The understanding is not the source, reason is of itself no spring of action. The understanding is but an instrument in the hand of the will. It is by hopes and fears that the ends of action are determined; all that reason does, is to find and determine the means." Or, as Hobbes more eloquently put it: "For the Thoughts, are to the Desires, as Scouts, and Spies, to range abroad, and find the way to the things Desired" (quoted in Gutmann, 1980, p. 21).

The Claim For Human Equality on the Basis of Shared Rationality

The second type of equality assumption identified by Gutmann takes a stronger view of the role of reason in human life. According to this view, all human beings are of equal moral worth by virtue of their shared capacity to rationally construct and follow a plan for their lives. Rationality is not an instrumental quality under this model, a mere organizer of our instinctual desires for wealth, power, and security. Rationality, rather, is a capacity to discern a higher moral law by reflecting on what John Locke and others have called the "state of nature" (1980, p. 8).[2] Human beings in Locke's state of nature live in a state of freedom and equality, and Locke reflects on the latter condition in the following way:

> All men are naturally in...a state...of equality, wherein all the power and jurisdiction is reciprocal, no one having more than another; there being nothing more evident than that creatures of the same species and rank, promiscuously born to all the same advantages of nature and the use of the same faculties should also be equal one amongst another without subordination or subjection... The state of nature has a law of nature to govern it, which obliges every one; and reason, which is that law, teaches all mankind who will but consult it that, being all equal and independent, no one ought to harm another in his life, health, liberty, or possessions. (1980, pp. 8-9; quoted also in Gutmann, 1980, p. 28)[3]

Immanuel Kant shares Locke's conviction—and, again, that of Hobbes before him, which many readers miss—that all men are moral equals of one another because they all possess the faculty of reason, which makes them unique among living things. Kant, however, traces out the implications of the equal rationality of persons in a manner that is especially helpful here. Whereas Locke connects man's status as a rational being mainly to the privilege of self-ownership—a notion of personal freedom that is peculiarly economic in nature—Kant connects man's rational capacity to a notion of individual dignity. For Kant, to possess the quality of rationality is to possess dignity, which requires, in turn, that one is treated in all cases—by both oneself and others—as an "end" and not as a means that is used for any purposes not freely chosen, however noble in intent. This is the meaning of Kant's "practical imperative," which is an extension of his more famous "categorical imperative." He articulates his practical imperative as follows: "Act in such a way that you always treat humanity, whether in your own person or in the person of any other, never simply as a means, but always at the same time as an end" (1964, p. 96).

From Description to Prescription:
Treating Persons as Equally Valuable

I switch now from a descriptive to a prescriptive posture, and to an examination of the way in which the classical liberal thinkers understood what it meant to treat individuals as equals in political practice. I have not yet applied labels to the thinkers referred to above, but have focused solely on the different ways that they justified their empirical claims that all persons possess roughly similar passions and intellectual faculties. Bentham and Mill were utilitarians; they defined utility, or usefulness, in terms of the pleasure an individual derives from satisfying her personal interests. They defined an individual's self-interest in an exclusively non-altruistic fashion, and assumed that—given economic scarcity and different entrepreneurial ambitions and talents across persons—no social order could please everyone.

Therefore, Bentham and Mill sought only to maximize the aggregate satisfaction of society as a whole—"the greatest good for the greatest number"—and assumed that the equality of persons was sufficiently respected if each person's interest counted equally in forming the aggregate, although only in purely formal, mathematical terms. Regarding negative liberty and economic opportunity for individuals, the utilitarians were pulled in two different directions. On one hand, they believed that individual wealth is of declining marginal utility—marginal economic gains satisfy poor persons more intensely than they do those who are already wealthy—and on that basis it can be argued that the level of aggregate satisfaction in society is maximized under an egalitarian economic model. On the other hand, given their assumption that individuals seek mainly to advance their own interests, the utilitarians thought that material inequality was an essential inducement to provoke ambitious, talented persons to utilize their gifts and to produce a greater pool of wealth for society as a whole. Equalizing economic opportunity, understood as an individual right in the negative sense, was seen as the logical way to bring this about. In actuality, the utilitarians did not take economic egalitarianism—the former option—very seriously; they were intoxicated with the promises of the free market and clearly supported negative economic liberty and its attendant material inequality over a more redistributive program.

At the same time, however, negative economic liberty—the right to possess the fruits of one's labor, to own private property, and to enjoy or exploit such property without intrusion by the state—is not perfectly secure under the utilitarian paradigm. Just as we saw in Chapter One—where it is explained that certain members of the business community support compensatory education programs for the poor not because these programs are seen as a moral right, but simply because they hope that these programs will turn otherwise ill-equipped laborers into those who add value to the American work force—the economic freedoms assigned to individuals under the historic utilitarian program are contingent upon the consequentialist calculus described above. It is hoped that by allowing these economic freedoms, and the material inequalities that they engender, society will end up richer in the aggregate than it would have been if these freedoms were not allowed. Locke and Kant, on the other hand, endow individual persons with a much firmer set of economic rights. Indeed, it is only under Locke's and Kant's theories that the economic prerogatives described here can accurately be called rights at all, as opposed to merely conditional privileges. Locke's ideas are more useful than Kant's in this regard because Locke speaks more explicitly about economic matters than Kant. Locke derived negative economic liberty directly from his principle of individual self-ownership; according to Locke, it is self-evident that each person owns herself, and from this fact it follows that she should have rights to the fruits of her labor, including any property which she has transformed in the process.

Yet, the point of this discussion is not to draw a detailed distinction between the utilitarians and the rights theorists, as I will refer to Locke and Kant. For my purposes, their similarities are far more important than their differences. Both sets of thinkers believe in the equal moral worth of persons, although they arrive at this conclusion from different paths. Both sets of thinkers recommend an economic system that honors negative liberty and formal equality of opportunity—the freedom to advance one's interests in a free market without interference from the state—although they endow such liberty with differing degrees of inviolability. My next task is to describe how contemporary liberal theorists have moved from the classical commitment to negative economic liberty—freedom from barriers to occupational success such as discrimination based on race or gender—to a commitment to positive economic liberty, which requires that all individuals are actually empowered to compete successfully in the free market. However, while they have significantly modified the classical liberal understanding of individual liberty and equality of opportunity, the contemporary revisionists have not forgotten one of the pillars of the liberal program: the classical commitment to the equal moral worth of persons. The contribution of the classical theorists in this regard cannot be overstated.

IV. The Contemporary Liberal Move to Positive Liberty and Substantive Equality of Opportunity

Contemporary Liberalism
and Positive Economic Liberty

The work of David G. Smith (1968) is helpful for understanding how classical liberal theory has been modified in recent times. Smith contends that it is the very success of classical liberalism that has stimulated the steady extension of its scope at the hands of late-nineteenth and twentieth-century revisionists. The institutionalization of the free market greatly enhanced the economic liberty of the bourgeois merchant-class, but most of the peasants and laborers were not in a position to take advantage of the changing opportunity structure. Thus, certain social critics—not surprisingly Karl Marx (1883) and later socialists such as R.H. Tawney (1931), but also English liberals such as T.H. Green (1888)—soon began to ask "What next?" or "Liberty for whom?" (Smith, p. 280). In order to make negative economic liberty truly effective for lower-class persons, these critics argued, the state needs to take more positive action in the form of public education or occupational training. Truly effective political liberties—and related civil liberties such as freedom of association or freedom of movement—are in fact dependent upon certain material prerequisites. It is not that the political and civil liberties themselves are illusory, but simply that they are not worth very much to those who do not possess the economic resources to exploit them. In John Rawls' words: "The inability to take advantage of one's rights and opportunities as a result of poverty and ignorance, and a lack of means generally, is sometimes counted among the constraints definitive of liberty.

I shall not, however, say this, but rather I shall think of these things as affecting the worth of liberty, the value to individuals of the rights that the [equal liberty] principle defines" (1971, p. 204). Another, more common way to characterize the difference between negative and positive economic liberty is to describe negative liberty as "freedom from" inappropriate barriers to economic success, as opposed to positive liberty, which represents the "freedom to" take advantage of economic opportunities because one has actually been empowered to do so.

As is often the case in social and political philosophy, the modern revisions to the classical model are in large part due to a change in historical conditions. While feudal society, by definition, was characterized by an inheritance-driven, socio-structural gulf between lords and serfs, the industrial revolution, along with the development of mass media and the freedom of the press, made the fact of centralized economic power—now in the form of the modern corporation—impossible to ignore. For instance, witness the sensational accounts of the notorious robber barons in the late nineteenth and early twentieth centuries, or the highly publicized exploitation of third-world labor by first-world corporations today. Although economic injustice is anything but new, it is now even more obvious than in the past that "one man's economic freedom is another man's oppression" (Smith, p. 280). Given the lopsided terms of competition between economic "have's" and "have-nots," contemporary liberals contend that it will require significant sacrifices on the part of the wealthy to create and sustain educational and occupational preparatory programs which will enable poor children to compete successfully in tomorrow's job market. This is to say nothing about the maintenance of a minimal safety net, or welfare state, to care for the needs of those who cannot adequately compete even if the terms of competition were made more fair. However, while sensitivity to the positive economic liberties of all persons requires both authentic equality of opportunity and a minimal welfare state, the focus of this project remains on the former. It is sufficient for my purposes here to define positive liberty as the actual capability to compete successfully for desirable occupational positions, over and against the simple absence of formal barriers.

Many scholars have asked whether contemporary liberalism, with its heavy emphasis on taxation in order to fund an array of expensive compensatory education and social welfare programs for the disadvantaged, is really still liberal at all. In Smith's words: "Liberty and equality, rights and powers are not the same things. Modern liberalism advocates collectivist means, invoking the state in aid of individuals and disadvantaged groups. It has adopted much of the program of democratic and socialist movements. Is modern liberalism still 'liberal'" (p. 281)? Before any "final" response to this question is possible, it will be necessary to distinguish between the interpretation of positive liberty discussed above and an even more aggressively egalitarian interpretation that I will introduce in the final section of this chapter. As for the conception of meritocracy advanced thus far, however, I think its liberal credentials are clear. Although it is true that significant transfers of wealth are necessary to create and maintain conditions of substantive equality of opportunity, the emphasis has remained on opportunity over and against results throughout the project. The contemporary liberal view simply represents a relatively newfound awareness of the magnitude of effort required to make individual autonomy a reality for all persons, as opposed to a merely formal right that for many people is of little actual value.[4]

The Structural and Economic Implications of Substantive Equality of Opportunity

As discussed in the opening chapter, the intuitive appeal of equal opportunity as a distributive principle is that it seeks to reconcile two simultaneously held, but seemingly incompatible moral and philosophical commitments: individual liberty and social equality. Regarding liberty specifically, the principle of equality of opportunity initially appeases those who prioritize individual economic freedom in that it does not directly require strict economic leveling as do more explicitly socialistic theories. However, if the empirical demands of substantive equality of opportunity are taken seriously, the distinction between equality of opportunity and equality of social conditions becomes much more fluid than is commonly supposed. Earlier this century, the prominent English Socialist R.H. Tawney reminded his liberal peers that merely equalizing access to schools and the workplace would not truly equalize occupational opportunities between the rich and the poor, and in Tawney's remarks one can see the shift from a negative to a positive understanding of liberty and opportunity:

> It is only the presence of a high degree of practical equality [equality of social conditions] which can diffuse and generalize opportunities to rise. Their existence in fact, and not merely in form, depends, not only upon an open road, but upon an equal start. It is precisely, of course, when capacity is aided by a high level of general well-being and culture in the milieu surrounding it, that its ascent is most likely to be regular and rapid, rather than fitful and intermittent. (1931, p. 128-129)

Three decades later, fellow-Englishman and analytical philosopher Bernard Williams articulated the same conceptual connection between equality of opportunity and a certain degree of equality of social conditions:

> One is not really offering equality of opportunity to Smith [an advantaged child] and Jones [a disadvantaged child] if one contents oneself with applying the same criteria to Smith and Jones...what one is doing there is to apply the same criteria to Smith as affected by favourable conditions and to Jones as affected by unfavourable but curable conditions. Here there is

a necessary pressure to equal up the conditions: to give *Smith* and *Jones* equality of opportunity involves regarding their conditions, where curable, as themselves part of what is done to Smith and Jones, and not part of Smith and Jones themselves.... This abstraction of persons in themselves from unequal environments is a way, if not of regarding them as equal, at least of moving recognizably in that direction, and is itself involved in equality of opportunity. (original emphases; 1962, p. 127-128)

The problematic ingredient within the mainstream liberal conception of equality of opportunity—formal, negative equality as characterized by equal access to educational and occupational competition—arises as generations succeed one another. In the hypothetical state of nature, a first generation exists which, by definition, begins life on equal material terms. However, the relative economic success of individuals within this first generation entails that their offspring experience large disparities regarding those material, cognitive, and affective resources that are commonly passed from parent to child. As Kenneth Strike puts it, "one generation's rewards are the next generation's opportunities" (1982, pp. 223). In order for the liberal theory of equality of opportunity to maintain legitimacy, Strike continues, liberal theory must surrender its assumption that "the social conditions of competition can be made distinct from society's reward structure...[and] equal opportunity should be interpreted as implying a constraint on the variance in social rewards permitted" (p. 225; see also Rawls, 1971). In other words, the realization of substantive equality of opportunity that endures over successive generations requires ongoing redistribution policies that prevent the outcome of economic competition in one generation from unduly influencing competition in the following generation. Citizens of an authentically meritocratic society must accept that the joy of hard work, recognizable success, and social influence are the proper rewards for expending their efforts and exercising their talents. A significant portion of their monetary rewards—much more than in the safety net programs characterizing the current American welfare state—will be lost to taxes which support social services benefiting children whose parents were less successful. It should be apparent at this point that the substantive interpretation of equality of opportunity is much more demanding than the formal interpretation, requiring significant and ongoing monetary sacrifices on the part of the affluent. Where the formal, negative conception of equal opportunity seeks only to ensure that the procedural workings of the free market are non-discriminatory, the substantive, positive conception requires continuous modifications of the results of market competition through transfer payments from the wealthy to the poor. As Strike correctly observes, the implications of equality of opportunity are quite radical in nature (1982; see also Bowles & Gintis, 1976).

Upon close inspection, some questions emerge from the preceding paragraph: How would tax revenues derived from the "winners" of occupational competition be used to support the children of their less fortunate peers? Exactly what social services would the equal opportunity society establish on behalf of children of the poor? These questions are important because one might respond that the taxes levied on successful persons are best conceived as simple transfer payments that less successful parents could employ at their own discretion, hopefully in ways that benefit their children. Assuming that a well-funded, progressive public education system existed, one could argue that this is as close as a society can get to setting the conditions necessary for fair occupational competition—allowing some inequality of income as an inducement to draw forth the best efforts of the most talented members of society, but preventing large discrepancies of wealth from accumulating as a result of individual differences in merit as measured by the market. Another solution that has been suggested is to leave the current American distributive system intact, but only after a massive, one-time redistribution of property and wealth (Krouse & McPherson, 1988). However, both of these suggestions are deficient because the most intractable inheritance-driven gaps in the preparation of children for the adult market-place are due to inequalities of human capital—those cognitive and affective resources that are passed on to children through family and community interactions—as opposed to physical capital, or money (see Kelley & Klein, 1981). Any social programs that seek to impact the life chances of poor children will focus on preparing them to compete in the market-place; while programs that meet basic physical needs such as nutrition and health care are inarguably necessary, these programs should be incorporated within a larger policy framework that has the development of human capital as its over-arching goal. Surely, public education is quite properly the lead institution in the development of human capital, but education should still be complemented by an array of other social services that have as their aim the nurturing of young persons so that they can survive, even thrive in the market-place upon adulthood.

I will leave to the final chapter the question of which combination of new human capital-oriented social services might best complement existing compensatory educational programs such as Head Start, Chapter One, Upward Bound, or other compensatory efforts on the part of individual states. However, I must immediately relate one crucial philosophical qualification regarding liberal efforts to establish an authentic meritocracy that endures across generations. James Fishkin (1983) points out that alleviating social inequalities related to attributes of human capital such as knowledge, skills, and attitudes is as dangerous for liberal theory as it is essential. For Fishkin, it is not only practically impossible to perfectly equalize educational resources provided to children of different family and community backgrounds, but at some point the effort itself becomes undesirable because it conflicts with the sacred liberal respect for the private sphere. The classic example of an illiberal attempt to perfectly equalize educational and occupational opportunity is Plato's recommendation in *The Republic* (1941) that all the children of Athens be removed from their homes and educated in public boarding schools. Fishkin is correct that the embeddedness of the nurturing processes within the private domains of family and community renders attempts to perfectly equalize human capital across social classes both impossible and morally problematic, and that liberalism itself becomes incoherent if the principle of equality of opportunity is pushed to the extreme. As stated throughout this book, the goal is to approximate equality of opportunity more fully than we do now, not to elevate some utopian conception of the perfectly egalitarian society.

V. An Examination of Criticisms of Meritocratic Equality of Opportunity

I have been speaking of economic liberty in meritocratic terms thus far, arguing that all persons should be equipped to compete successfully in the market-place, and that one measure of success we might look for is an increasing proportionality of representation across ethnic and gender groups at all occupational levels. I have assumed throughout this book that inequalities in status and wealth within and across these social groups that are a result of truly fair occupational competition are perfectly legitimate. In the following section, however, I will introduce three prominent thinkers who have questioned the moral defensibility of meritocracy itself, no matter how authentically fair it is. While these thinkers acknowledge that attaching social rewards such as important occupational positions—and their accompanying income and social status—to individual achievement is more justifiable than attaching these rewards to hereditary identity, they argue that a meritocratic social order carries with it its own set of problems. As an interpretation of what it means to treat human beings equally—the moral and philosophical core of liberal political theory—meritocratic equality of opportunity is held by these critics to be a laudable half-step forward from the inheritance-driven feudal regime, but just that: a half-step. Before concluding the chapter, I must respond to this criticism of meritocratic equality of opportunity if the thesis of this project is to be convincing.

Michael Young's Fictional Critique of Meritocracy

The term "meritocracy" was first used by Michael Young in his innovative fictional satire of British civil service and education reform, *The Rise of the Meritocracy: 1870-2033* (1958). Using the British reforms of the late nineteenth and twentieth century as his foil—where inherited privilege was replaced by individual achievement as the central means of advancement—Young exposed the dark side of Jefferson's vision of a natural aristocracy. The dominant force behind meritocratic reform in Britain was not egalitarian or democratic, but purely utilitarian in the sense that social productivity was the highest value:

> The rate of social progress depends upon the degree to which power is matched with intelligence. The Britain of a century ago squandered its resources by condemning even talented people to manual work.... But Britain could not be a caste society if it was to survive as a great nation, great that is, in comparison with others. To withstand inter-national competition the country had to make better use of its human material, above all, of the talent which even in England...[was] too scarce.... The proportion of people with I.Q.'s over 130 could not be raised...but the proportion of such people in work which called upon their full capacities was steadily raised. (Young, p. 12)

Young understood the tenuous status of equality of opportunity under the utilitarian paradigm, and he presented the principle of equal opportunity as a brilliant invention that enabled the meritocrats to masquerade their utilitarian intentions as a commitment to social equality. Young also understood that the glorification of increasing aggregate wealth masked severe and increasing inequalities of wealth and prestige between individuals. What the egalitarians ignored, he declares, was that "as it was applied in practice, equality of opportunity meant equality of opportunity to become unequal" (p. 103).

John Schaar's Philosophical Critique of Equality of Opportunity

Explicitly following Young, John Schaar has advanced a non-fictional, philosophical critique of the meritocratic principle in a now famous essay entitled "Equality of Opportunity and Beyond" (1967). Schaar understands the sacredness of his target; recall from Chapter One that he describes equal opportunity as "far and away the dominant conception of equality in the public mind...so entrenched as to be an atmospheric condition" (p. 167, p. 239). Schaar seconds Young's observation that the equal opportunity principle is misleading, apparently defending equality while really defending the right to become unequal. He contrasts equality of opportunity with a "genuinely democratic understanding of equality" (p. 236), which does not tolerate oligarchy of any kind, even an oligarchy defined by individual merit. Schaar is not criticizing hierarchical organization in industry or government per se—where individuals in leadership positions perform special functions and receive special rewards; any non-utopian society must rely on certain inducements to entice its most talented members to exercise their gifts in ways that promote the common good. What Schaar criticizes, rather, is the hyper-hierarchical, hyper-competitive mode of thinking where authority implies sole possession of competency. A truly democratic society, Schaar submits, strives for the broadest possible sharing of responsibility and power, and the competitive individualism that over-zealous meritocracies exalt can only detract from such an endeavor. In Schaar's words:

> Of course there must be hierarchy, but that does not imply a hierarchical and bureaucratic mode of thinking and acting. It need imply no more than specialization of function. Similarly, the fact that complexity demands specialization of function does not imply the unique merit and authority of those who perform the special functions. On the contrary: A full appreciation of complexity implies the need for the widest possible diffusion of knowledge, sharing of views, and mutual acceptance of responsibility by all members of the affected community. (p. 240)

John Rawls' Alternative Theory of Distributive Justice

Finally, explicitly relying upon both Young and Schaar, John Rawls (1971) published *A Theory of Justice*, the most widely-known critique of meritocratic equality of opportunity. Like Young, Rawls rejects the utilitarian defense of meritocratic equal opportunity in particular:

> This [meritocratic] form of social order...uses equality of opportunity as a way of releasing men's energies in the pursuit of economic prosperity and political dominion. There exists a marked disparity between the upper and lower classes in both means of life and rights and privileges of organizational authority. The culture of the poorer strata is impoverished while that of the governing and technocratic elite is securely based on the service of the national ends of power and wealth. Equality of opportunity means an equal chance to leave the less fortunate behind in the personal quest for influence and social position. (p. 107)

Rawls' debt to Schaar is equally clear. Echoing Schaar's objection that the competitive, hierarchical nature of meritocracy detracts from a genuinely democratic mentality, Rawls sets forth his own "democratic" corrective to the traditional liberal model (1971, p. 75). Yet, it is immediately important to clarify that under Rawls' democratic conception of distributive justice, the principle of equal opportunity is not discarded, but only qualified. Rawls' understanding of the traditional liberal ideal is similar to the substantive interpretation advanced here: "In all sectors of society there should be roughly equal prospects of culture and achievement for everyone similarly motivated and endowed. The expectations of those with the same abilities and aspirations should not be affected by their social class" (p. 73).

While Rawls supports the substantive model as far as it goes, he identifies one significant inconsistency. Essentially, Rawls—along with some others such as Ronald Dworkin (1981) and Amartya Sen (1992)—does not see why inequalities of life chances that arise from social contingencies such as race or class are any more morally problematic than those that arise from a natural endowment like talent. On what basis do we decide to mitigate inequality of opportunities related to social position, but fully accept that the naturally gifted will go farther in life than those less talented? For Rawls, both social and natural attributes are "arbitrary from a moral point of view," and to equalize opportunities related to the former but not the latter is arbitrary as well (p. 72). Again, Rawls does not reject the meritocratic approach to distributive justice upon identifying its shortcomings, but simply qualifies it. He qualifies the meritocratic approach by placing the principle of equal opportunity within a more comprehensive theory of justice that allows it to operate while simultaneously correcting for what he believes to be its failings.

Rawls' influential theory, which he calls "justice as fairness" (p. 11), has served as a springboard for a whole host of political philosophers who have pushed the egalitarian edges of liberal theory. The conviction that guides these aggressively egalitarian liberals is that meritocratic equality of opportunity is a "necessary, but not sufficient" principle of distributive justice, to borrow a phrase from Nicholas Burbules and Ann L. Sherman's discussion of equal educational opportunity (1979, p. 105; see also Howe, 1989). According to these thinkers, the treatment of persons as equals entails even more than substantial and ongoing human capital-related investments in the youth of a given society; the treatment of persons as equals entails that for the duration of any given person's life, social prestige and material rewards should reflect her choices and effort more than her actual achievement level (Kymlicka, 1990). Ronald Dworkin articulates this position quite nicely. Dworkin asserts, in Kymlicka's paraphrasing, that differences in material and social well-being should solely be a product of an individual's choices, rather than being dependent on her actual accomplishments, which are in some part a function of what Rawls calls the "natural lottery" of talent (1971, p. 74). Consequently, Dworkin recommends a distributive system that is simultaneously "ambition sensitive" and "endowment [in]sensitive" (1981, p. 311).

A Response to the Criticisms of Meritocracy and Equality of Opportunity

Before proceeding to address the critiques of meritocratic equality of opportunity advanced above, I want to make my strategy clear. I am generally sympathetic to each of these critiques and will not refute them. As stated in the opening chapter, I am aware that the concepts of meritocracy and equality of opportunity mean different things to different people, and are also likely to be advocated with different degrees of sincerity. Young, Schaar, and Rawls are not attacking straw men; many thinkers and political actors have championed the very ideas that they find objectionable (see, i.e. Bell, 1972). But

I do not think the vision of authentic meritocracy advanced here is guilty of the offenses that Young and Schaar identify, and I think this vision is compatible with parts of the Rawlsian program. Upon completing this section, one might ask: if the critics addressed here do not directly challenge your thesis, so that it is possible to simply agree with them or show how their ideas are compatible with your own, then do they need to be addressed at all? I believe they do. While the main impact of this detour might be to prevent readers from naively assuming that the benefits of meritocracy are beyond dispute, this is sufficient justification. The idea of authentic meritocracy captures much of what I am trying to convey in this book, and anyone who chooses to push these ideas further should be aware of the differing perceptions that people have about the term itself.

The clearest way to respond to the critiques reviewed above is to address them one by one. As for Young's fictional critique, he is right to satirize the utilitarian rationale for equality of opportunity as it first emerged in late nineteenth-century England and has no doubt been employed in many places since then. Actually, the utilitarian rationale for meritocracy is not so much wrong as incomplete. The feudal practice of granting important positions to persons on the basis of birthright surely meant that many dull individuals were "in over their heads," and widening the channels of opportunity has undoubtedly increased the talent pool available for such positions. However, as explained in section three above, a utilitarian foundation for equality of opportunity is tenuous, and the rationale advanced in this project is much more solid, depending on inviolable rights that are accorded to all individuals on the basis of their moral status as human beings. In fact, the substantive interpretation of equal opportunity will likely conflict with the utilitarian desire to maximize aggregate wealth because increasing taxes for corporations and individuals often provokes dis-investment and a shrinking economy, in the short-term at least. But as the previous discussion of Strike's work made clear, this is what the substantive vision requires. In order to prevent the results of economic competition in one generation from unduly influencing competition in the following generation, significant and continuous transfer payments are necessary to fund human-capital development programs that compensate for parents' differing abilities—due either to unequal competence or unequal resources—to prepare their children to compete in the marketplace. These transfer payments are necessary because children born into unfortunate circumstances deserve them, regardless of their impact on aggregate wealth. The foundation of equal opportunity advanced in this project is rights-based and attends to individuals rather than societies. Young is right to be suspicious of an utilitarian basis for equal opportunity, but I do not make this mistake here.

My response to Schaar is very similar to my response to Young. Schaar is right that modern capitalistic societies tend to be hyper-individualistic and hyper-competitive in character, and that the assumption that equal opportunity exists can exacerbate a cultural tendency to label the poor as self-evidently incompetent. However, these attitudinal and relational problems are not logically attached to the principle of equality of opportunity itself, but rather to the ethos of capitalistic societies in which the ideal is popular. As Charles A. Tesconi and Emanuel Hurwitz, Jr. point out, equality of opportunity is a "second-order principle" that is compatible with a wide variety of economic systems, not just capitalistic but socialistic and mixed economies as well. Consequently, it should not be too easily blamed for deficiencies in the broader system in which it operates. What I mean to communicate is that Schaar raises important concerns about meritocracy as it is often celebrated in the United States and other capitalistic countries. However, I do not think that these concerns follow inevitably from my conception of authentic meritocracy. I do not present substantive equality of opportunity as a self-sufficient principle of justice for modern societies, but merely as one piece of the good society, a piece that simply seeks to ensure that educational and occupational competition are not inappropriately corrupted by irrelevant ascriptive characteristics such as racial and ethnic identity or socio-economic status. Rawls, however, does present a comprehensive theory of distributive justice, and I now wish to demonstrate that my argument for substantive equality of opportunity—which is both limited in scope and profoundly important at the same time—is compatible with his more comprehensive program.

As described above, while Rawls admires the substantive interpretation of equality of opportunity because it decrees that an individual's life prospects should not be unduly influenced by social attributes like race or socio-economic status, he does not see why a person's natural talents are any less arbitrary. Thus, a meritocratic system that attaches social rewards to ability as determined in the free market cannot stand alone, and must be integrated into a larger distributive scheme that protects persons who, through no fault of their own, are less talented than others. I will not address all three parts of what Rawls calls his "special conception" of justice (p. 151), but just the "opportunity principle"—which is tantamount to substantive equal opportunity—and the "difference principle," with the former having priority over the latter (p. 75). Assuming that authentic equality of opportunity has been obtained and would not be threatened (the opportunity principle), Rawls argues that social and economic institutions should be arranged in whatever manner would predictably result in the highest material well-being for the least advantaged citizens (the difference principle). Now, the question of which economic system—capitalism, socialism, or something in-between—best fulfills Rawls' difference principle has been debated for almost three decades, but for simplicity's sake I will limit my remarks to a capitalist-welfare state context like the United States. Given this context, Rawls' theory provides strong justification for a healthy safety net for those who, for reasons related to mental or physical deficits, are unable to contribute valuably in the work-place. Rawls' theory could also support Strike's requirement that the variation in wages between talented and less talented persons be kept small so that these differences do not impact the opportunities of their children, although this ends up being an empirical economic debate which I will avoid here. The policy implications of Rawls' belief in the arbitrariness of unequal natural endowments do not clash with those stemming from the conception of substantive equality of opportunity advanced in this project.

Although it might be enough to simply admit that my vision of authentic meritocracy is not a self-sufficient principle of distributive justice and requires a side-constraint such as that provided by Rawls' difference principle, I think I can fold my argument even more neatly into Rawls' theory of justice. Since I admire Rawls' work a great deal, I will take this opportunity. I believe that K-12 education, as the primary instrument of equalizing occupational opportunities in our society, fits nicely into Rawls' opportunity principle. If this is true, and if a difference principle exists which softens the impact of meritocracy on under-talented individuals, then an education system that helps create authentic meritocracy requires no apologies. Our main responsibility is to make the occupational and economic "race" fair when it begins in high school or upon graduation. But this last phrase is of utmost importance. Until the time that students enter college, or at least until they enter high school, education should not be strictly meritocratic itself.

VI. Conclusion:
Substantive Equality of Opportunity and Treating Persons as Equals

My aim in the preceding discussion has been to lay out my conception of substantive equality of opportunity as clearly as possible, and to support this conception by demonstrating its continuity with certain elements of the liberal tradition in political philosophy. More specifically, I have reviewed the claims for the equal moral worth of persons and negative liberty as they emerged in the classical liberal tradition, and the way in which modern liberals have recognized that liberty is better conceived as a positive principle, the "freedom to" as opposed the mere "freedom from." My vision of substantive equality of opportunity is an expression of positive liberty: social institutions—schools in particular—should be arranged so that all children are prepared to go as far in life as their native abilities and willingness to work allow. While I am very supportive of a significant social safety net for persons with mental or physical deficits that impede their ability to compete in the free market, these policies are not relevant to the conduct of K-12 education, at least outside the realm of Special Education. One of the main purposes of K-12 education is to prepare students for meritocratic competition upon adulthood. While the first eight, perhaps even twelve, years of education itself should not be meritocratic in design, the ultimate meritocratic purpose that schools serve requires no apology.

In conclusion, I wish to underscore what I believe to be the most important claim in this chapter: that the substantive interpretation of equal opportunity honors the equal moral worth of persons, whereas the formal interpretation does not. Again, the equal moral worth of persons was the most important discovery of classical liberals such as Locke, Kant, and the utilitarians. They conferred this equality on the basis of descriptive characteristics of persons such as roughly equal passions and the capacity for rationality. Another way to describe the equal moral worth of persons is to speak of equal dignity, a conviction which Kant held and which George Kateb (1994) recently echoed when he stated that all people are equal in "unearned human dignity" (p. 529). However, while the classical liberals' recognition of the dignity of all persons represents a great advance over their feudal predecessors, their understanding of the implications of human equality was not yet complete. As demonstrated above, negative liberty and formal equality of opportunity are not worth much if a person does not possess the social and material pre-requisites to take advantage of such liberty. As Rawls said, it is not the possession of an abstract right to liberty, but the concrete worth of such liberty that matters.

The claim that formal equality of opportunity does not sufficiently respect human dignity can be illustrated in a brief vignette. Suppose we were to travel to an inner-city neighborhood and speak with one of the children that Jonathan Kozol describes in *Amazing Grace: The Lives of Children and the Conscience of a Nation* (1996). Suppose this child is underfed, spends a majority of her time alone because her father is gone and her mother works two low-paying jobs, and attends a dilapidated elementary school in which she is grouped with other "low-ability" children who, like her, do not receive much academic help at home. Suppose we look her in the eyes and proceed to explain to her that we are working to reduce overt race and gender-based discrimination in schools and the work-place, but beyond that she must somehow find the will to make it on her own. It would help if she could find mentors to help her along the way, but that is not a public responsibility. Do we really believe this child can make it on her own, even if overt discrimination has been reduced? Can we say that we are sufficiently respecting this child's moral worth, or her dignity?

The answer is no. In order to honor this child's dignity, we need to go well beyond protecting her negative freedoms. Since she did not choose her impoverished position in society, we owe it to her to alleviate as much as possible the impact these conditions will have on her life prospects. The substantive conception of equality of opportunity, with its attendant commitment to positive liberty, provides the philosophical rationale for doing so. According to this conception, individuals are being treated as equals when their chances of educational and occupational success are truly equal to that of their peers, independent of their native ability and willingness to work. They might not always be treated equally by the meritocratic institutions they encounter as adults, but over the course of their lives they should be treated as equals. The distinction is important. I turn now to an examination of the way in which equality of opportunity has been operationalized in American educational policy.

Notes

1. "Liber" means "free."
2. The state of nature can be understood as a hypothetical moment in history before formal civilization occurred. This philosophical creation is meant to tease out a person's true relationship to her environment and to humanity by peeling back any effects of history that have distorted these relationships (see also Hobbes, 1962; Rousseau, 1988).
3. Please forgive the gender-exclusive language in this section. It is the language used by these early liberal thinkers, and I have chosen to leave it as is.
4. The philosophical literature on negative and positive liberty is more complicated than the discussion above implies. I have focused on economic matters alone, arguing mainly that persons deserve

more than the mere absence of interference, but should be positively equipped in some way to take advantage of their negative liberty. Isaiah Berlin (1969), who popularized the distinction, actually dwells more on the dangers of positive liberty than its virtues. Berlin rightly understands that if negative liberty is forsaken for a purely positive conception, then paternalist policies can be advocated that "equip" people for economic and political participation in new utopian societies, regardless of their own desires. Stalinist Communism is perhaps the classic example of a regime that grossly violated negative human freedoms, even the right to life, in the name of a utopian vision of positive freedom for all people. My aim is to hold the two types of freedom in productive tension, recognizing the value of both. Finally, certain philosophers reject the distinction between negative and positive freedom in favor of a unified conception that encompasses both values simultaneously (see Cohen, 1960; MacCallum, 1967), but for my purposes the distinction is useful.

Chapter Four

Opportunities To Learn:
The Manifestations
of Equality of Opportunity
in American Educational Policy

I. Chapter Preview

This chapter has four objectives. I first will trace the evolution of the concept of equal educational opportunity from the early days of the American republic to the present time, culminating in the substantive, results-oriented interpretation that was first articulated by James Coleman in the 1960s and further developed by several educational philosophers who followed him. I then will examine federal educational policy since the 1960s in order to assess the degree to which policy-makers have been able to implement equal educational opportunity policies in concrete and sustainable ways. Given the obvious tension between national leadership concerning K-12 education and the constitutional mandate of states to take the lead in such matters, it is necessary to examine recent efforts to address equity issues at the state level as well, which is my third objective. The discussions of federal and state-level educational policy will focus on the presence and scope of "school delivery standards"— now more commonly called "opportunity-to-learn standards"—

alongside curricular content and student performance standards as targets of recent standards-based reform efforts. In the final section of the chapter, I will consider in more detail the potential of opportunity-to-learn standards for operationalizing equality of educational opportunity.

II. Evolving Beliefs and Assumptions About the Role of Schools in Equalizing Opportunity

Public Schooling as the "Great Equalizer"

As citizens of a liberal and meritocratic state, Americans have always perceived public education as a ladder which the ablest children of all backgrounds can climb toward occupational and economic success. Thomas Jefferson dreamed of replacing the existing aristocracy of inherited privilege with a "natural aristocracy" of talent (letter to John Adams; anthologized in Barber & Battistoni, 1993, p. 41). In his "Bill for the More General Diffusion of Knowledge in the State of Virginia," Jefferson outlined a plan that called for three years of elementary education for all children and scholarships to grammar schools, and eventually the University of Virginia, to the most promising working-class boys. Jefferson supported equalizing educational opportunity mainly because he believed that natural talent was more deserving of reward than privileged birth, but he supported mass education on utilitarian grounds as well. He believed that society would run more efficiently when important positions were filled by the truly gifted rather than the merely well-born. When his bill was defeated in the Virginia state legislature in 1817, a disappointed Jefferson lamented that his colleagues did not "generally possess information enough to perceive the important truths, that knowledge is power, that knowledge is safety, that knowledge is happiness" (quoted in Hechinger, 1976, p. 1).

By the middle of the nineteenth century, elitist resistance to Jefferson's democratizing impulse for education was weakening. Horace Mann, a reform-minded legislator and school system administrator in Massachusetts, was the new "high priest of a growing faith in education that fell little short of a new religion" (Hechinger, p. 2). Mann saw education as the single most powerful tool with which to erase rigid class distinctions:

> If education be equally diffused, it will draw property after it, by the strongest of all attractions; for such a thing never did happen, as that an intelligent and practical body of men should be permanently poor. Property and labor, in different classes, are essentially antagonistic; but property and labor, in the same class, are essentially fraternal.... Education, then, beyond all other devices of human origin, is the great equalizer of the conditions of men—the balance-wheel of the social machinery. (quoted in Hechinger, p. 3)

More than a century later, President Lyndon Johnson espoused a similar quasi-religious faith in education as the remedy for socio-economic inequality:

> Onto my desk each day come the problems of 190 million men and women. When we consider those problems, when we study them, when we analyze them, when we evaluate what can be done, the answer almost always comes down to one word: education. This is true for economic problems, this is true for social problems. (quoted in Hayes, 1968, p. 86)

It was the Johnson administration (1963-1969) that initiated compensatory programs like Head Start and Chapter One that were discussed earlier. Unlike his nineteenth-century predecessors, Johnson included blacks and native Americans in his vision of equalizing educational opportunity. He recognized that improving education for minority children was one of the nation's principal unfinished tasks (Kantor & Lowe, 1995).

However, before we heroize Johnson, it quickly should be noted that Johnson's educational programs were quite inexpensive in relation to more directly egalitarian programs involving health insurance or income redistribution. A more socialistic agenda had made a strong run in this country following the great depression of the 1930s, but business interests prevailed over labor interests in Congress throughout the World War II period, and what became known as "welfare state capitalism" in postwar politics was a far cry from the Socialists' vision. Consequently, when officials in the Johnson administration formulated poverty policy, they considered more aggressive welfare reforms like income redistribution and national health insurance politically unfeasible and turned instead to education as their major tool of social reform. Johnson did sincerely believe that education was a weapon against poverty, but his Horace Mann-esque rhetoric about the sufficiency of schooling for social mobility undoubtedly had another purpose: it aimed to conceal his compromise with business and congressional interests regarding the scope of the welfare state (Kantor & Lowe, 1995).

The Recent Reappraisal
of the Power of Schools

Ironically, it was Johnson's alleged faith in education that set in motion a chain of events that sobered Americans' confidence in public education as the great equalizer. Johnson's Civil Rights Act of 1964 called for a survey and report on "the lack of availability of equal educational opportunities for individuals by reason of race, color, religion, or national origin" in public education (Aaron, 1978, p. 75). The *Equality of Educational Opportunity Survey* (1966), constructed by a team led by James Coleman, was one of the largest social science surveys ever conducted. The Coleman Report, as the survey analysis came to be called, performed two functions. First, it summarized data on the major resource variables such as facilities, curricula, and teacher quality available to black and white students across the country. Second, it reported statistical analyses relating these input variables and other student characteristics to black and white students' performances on standardized tests (Aaron, p. 76). Actually, the Coleman Report assessed the degree of educational opportunity for several racial groups besides whites and blacks. Yet, the relationship between schooling opportunities for black and white students was the most politicized educational issue during the Great Society period, and the summary statements in the Coleman Report reflect this preoccupation with black-white comparisons.

Regarding the data on school inputs such as facilities, curricula, and teacher quality, everyone—including Coleman himself—was surprised to find that only small differences in resources existed between schools attended by blacks and whites. Regarding the correlations between the traditional input variables and students' performance on standardized tests, the results were equally surprising, but in this case devastating as well. As expected, blacks scored very low in comparison with whites. Yet, since blacks and whites were not generally exposed to schools of differing resource levels, their differences in cognitive performance could not be attributed to input inequalities. Coleman attributed their inferior performance to something that had very little to do with traditional school input: the family backgrounds of fellow students. In Coleman's own words:

> It is interesting to note that this examination of the relation of school inputs to effects on achievement showed that those input characteristics of schools that are most alike for Negroes and whites have least effect on their achievement. The magnitudes of differences between schools attended by Negroes and those attended by whites were as follows: least, facilities and curriculum; next, teacher quality; and greatest, educational backgrounds of fellow students. The order of importance of

these inputs on the achievement of Negro [and white] students
is precisely the same: facilities and curriculum least, teacher
quality next, and backgrounds of fellow students, most.
(Coleman, 1968, p. 20)

The Coleman Report triggered a slew of other studies, most
notably Christopher Jencks' (et al.) *Inequality* (1972) and the
Rand Corporation's *How Effective is Schooling* (1972). These
studies generally confirmed Coleman's claim that the family
backgrounds of students—a variable that was designed to capture racial, economic, cultural, and community impacts on the
cognitive development of children—exercised a far greater influence on children's scholastic achievement than their schooling
experiences. As the Rand study concluded: "There is good reason
to ask whether our educational problems are, in fact, school
problems. The most profitable line of attack on educational
problems may not, after all, be through the schools" (Averch et
al., 1972, p. vii). In anecdotal reference to a quip that a Harvard
scholar reportedly made to a colleague upon reviewing the
Coleman Report, these studies have come to be known collectively as the "schools don't make a difference" research.

Looking back a quarter-century later, it is difficult to appre-
ciate the cataclysmic impact that the "schools don't make a
difference" research had on the educational establishment at
that time. This is true for two reasons. First, from a contemporary perspective, it is apparent that the studies are methodologi-
cally immature. Only Coleman's methodology is critiqued here,
but the others have very similar flaws. Coleman's thesis—that
the coexistence of equal school resources and unequal scholastic
achievement for blacks and whites demonstrates that schools
possess little educative power relative to family background—
was based on snapshot data. Snapshot data cannot adequately
take into account any changes in the relationship between
variables that have occurred prior to the time of analysis. Given
that the study was done little more than a decade after the

Supreme Court's desegregation mandate (*Brown v. Topeka*, 1954), this is a significant shortcoming. Also, the large size of Coleman's survey limited the kind of information that could be procured. The survey focused solely on between-school differences and did not examine the ways in which blacks and whites experienced the same school in different ways. The effects of tracking, for instance, were not addressed; nor were the more subtle ways in which blacks and whites experience the same instruction in the same classroom differently. Finally, standardized test scores were the only measures of cognitive achievement used. Athough standardized tests are very useful, no written test can completely capture a child's intellectual growth, and some argue that most tests are biased in favor of white, middle class students as well (Aaron, 1978).

Second, educators have simply gotten used to the idea that schools cannot equalize educational opportunity on their own. Despite the methodological flaws of the research of the 1960s and 1970s, the negative conclusion that schools are not overcoming educational inequalities stemming from non-school sources has held true. Regarding racial disparities in educational achievement—on which the Coleman study focused—longitudinal studies such as the ongoing National Assessment of Educational Progress (NAEP) project show that the reading, writing, and mathematics skills of black and Hispanic children have continued to lag significantly behind those of whites. Regarding socioeconomic disparities in educational achievement, family background characteristics such as the parents' income and educational attainment continue to exercise a strong influence on the academic success of children (National Education Longitudinal Study [NELS], 1988; NAEP, 1985; Natriello et al., 1990). Regarding differences in educational attainment across social groups— which is perhaps the more important variable given that educational credentials are more clearly correlated with job success than cognitive ability as measured by standardized tests (Blaug,

1972; Collins, 1971, 1979; Jencks, 1985)—similar inequalities exist. After reviewing the literature concerning the relationship between social class and educational attainment, Kathleen P. Bennett and Margaret D. LeCompte (1990) draw the following conclusion: "The most powerful predictor of how much education individuals obtained was the social class background of their parents, as measured by their income level, occupation, and education" (quoted in Knapp & Woolverton, 1995, p. 552).

Again, the methodological failings of the "schools don't make a difference" research do not discount the fact that their central thesis turned out to be correct: the American educational system—taken as a whole—does not significantly reduce the effects of educational inequalities among children that arise from non-school sources such as family and community; in fact, many social reproduction theorists argue that, far from alleviating the problem, our educational system exacerbates it (Baratz & Baratz, 1970; Bowles & Gintis, 1976; Bourdieu & Passeron, 1977). As Henry Aaron describes below, this reality presents a problem for the United States' claim to be a liberal meritocracy:

> The "findings" of the Coleman Report were consistent with either a conservative or a radical view of American society, but not with a liberal one. Conservatives could point to the apparent dominant influence of social class and claim that differences lie within the family and cannot be reduced by socially acceptable intervention, that the large amount of unexplained variation in test scores is genetic in origin, or that we were simply ignorant about the determinants of academic performance and should do nothing; in any case, the present order is more or less unchangeable. Radicals could claim that the order is determined through political power and class conflict and that schools merely replicate the pattern of power and of aspiration found in the existing generation. For liberals, the findings were devastating because they denied the possibility of instrumental change. (Aaron, 1978, p. 77)

Two Different Responses to the Recent Reappraisal

In order to set the stage for a discussion about defining equal educational opportunity for purposes of assessing its presence in a particular society, I wish to briefly review the different ways in which Coleman and Jencks—the major architects of the "schools don't make a difference" research—responded to their disappointing findings. It is fascinating to note that in the early stages of their careers both Coleman and Jencks were quite optimistic about the prospects of equalizing occupational opportunity through education (see Jencks, 1992, p. 6). By the time he wrote *Inequality*, however, Jencks had lost his faith in education as a tool of egalitarian reform. Believing that formal education did little to counteract the cognitive effects of family background inequalities, Jencks proposed a more direct route to distributive equality. He recommended that taxation policy be made more aggressively redistributive, rather than futilely waiting for educational reform to produce economic equality in some distant generation.

Coleman's research drove him to the same conclusion about the power of education—as then practiced—to counter-balance family background inequalities, but he responded differently. Coleman resisted Jencks' inclination to "throw in the towel" concerning an education-driven meritocracy and to resort to economic leveling through direct transfer programs. He criticized Jencks' ideological move from equality of opportunity to equality of results through redistributive taxation because he felt it failed to respect the fundamental human need to earn rewards for oneself:

> The decision to make social investments in equality of result rather than equality of opportunity is predicated on the assumption that there are no satisfactions that derive from opportunity and achievement—that all satisfactions derive from consumption of the social product. Only if money income

and the consumption it allows were the source of all satisfaction would this assumption be correct. Yet we know that it is not. Much satisfaction, perhaps most, arises from the achievement of certain internally-set goals, from the capability to overcome obstacles. Only by increasing opportunity, by investing in the personal resources that provide this capability, can these satisfactions be increased. (Coleman, 1973, p. 136)

Coleman understood that perfect equality of educational opportunity was an unattainable ideal. However, while he knew that all we can ever hope for is "a reduction in inequality" of educational opportunity rather than perfect equality (Coleman, 1975, p. 29), Coleman did not for this reason reject the ideal. On the contrary, he refined the standard for measuring its fulfillment in practice, making explicit the historic, vague assumptions about the power of schools to serve students of all social backgrounds equally well.

Prior to the Coleman study, academics and policy-makers typically assessed the degree to which equality of educational opportunity existed by examining major input variables such as instructional facilities, curriculum materials, and teacher quality. While in the process of carrying out the *Equality of Educational Opportunity* study, Coleman proposed what philosophers would call a "consequentialist," results-oriented alternative to the traditional formulation: measuring the presence or absence of equal educational opportunity by the equalization over time of average academic achievement between children of different racial and socio-economic groups. Actually, this new proposal and the related empirical findings reviewed above received only moderate space within the Coleman Report as a whole, but these sections generated disproportionate interest. Also, two years after the publication of the Coleman Report, the principal author reflected on the implications of his results-oriented approach in more detail. His remarks are worth quoting at length:

By making the dichotomy between inputs and results explicit, and by focusing attention not only on inputs but on results, the

Report brought into the open what had been underlying all the concepts of equality of educational opportunity but had remained largely hidden: that the concept implied *effective* equality of opportunity, that is, equality in those elements that are effective for learning.... The controversy that has surrounded the Report indicates that measurement of effects is still subject to sharp disagreement, but the crucial point is that effects of inputs have come to constitute the basis for assessment of school quality (and thus equality of opportunity) in place of using certain inputs by definition as measures of quality (e.g., small classes are better than large, higher-paid teachers are better than lower-paid ones, by definition)...

The implication of the most recent concept [equal educational results across racial and socio-economic groups], as I have described it, is that the responsibility to create achievement lies with the educational institution, not the child. The difference in achievement at grade 12 between the average Negro and the average white is, in effect, the degree of inequality of opportunity, and the reduction of that inequality is the responsibility of the school. This shift in responsibility follows logically from the change in the concept of equality of educational opportunity from school resource inputs to effects of schooling. (original emphasis; Coleman, 1968, p. 21, 24)

Coleman was on the right track; educational rhetoric in the tradition of Jefferson, Mann, and Johnson often implied that children's total educational opportunities—those arising from family, community, and school—can be equalized by the powerful educative effects of formal schooling. Regardless of whether or not schools could actually deliver on this promise, the equal results standard—equal achievement across different racial and socio-economic groups—was clearly truer to the American attitude toward education than was equal inputs. Of course, no one was expecting that schools produce equal scholastic achievement for all individuals or for all individuals within any particular group; given the obvious differences among persons in ability and aspirations, this is an impossible and even undesirable standard.

Defining Equality of Educational Opportunity After Coleman

Several educational philosophers (Green, 1971; Gutmann, 1987; Howe, 1989; Strike, 1988) have sought to refine Coleman's proposed equal results standard. The work of Kenneth Strike and Thomas Green is particularly useful for my purposes here. At the heart of the principle of equal educational opportunity, Strike contends, lies the requirement that an individual's educational and occupational success should depend only on "morally relevant characteristics" such as effort and ability, rather than on irrelevant characteristics such as race or gender (p. 155). Again, assuming that the potential to sustain effort and succeed is unrelated to these irrelevant characteristics, then a comparison of any two groups differentiated by such characteristics should approximate what Green calls "group parity" (p. 87). Green defines group parity as a condition in which the range of differences in educational achievement across racial and socioeconomic groups, and the distribution of achievement within that range, are roughly equivalent.

Regarding its conceptual coherence, the equal results standard for assessing equality of educational opportunity has "taken a bit of a philosophical beating" (Howe, 1989, p. 317; for criticisms of the results standard, see Page, 1976; Burbules, Lord, & Sherman, 1982; Burbules & Sherman, 1990). The criticisms essentially boil down to the objection that a results standard for measuring equality of educational opportunity is conceptually unfeasible because opportunities, by definition, entail choices on the part of recipients, and social institutions cannot properly be held accountable for how much people make of their opportunities. Kenneth Howe (1989) creatively defends the equal results standard. He concedes the conceptual difficulty in the case of adults because most adults are mature enough to be held responsible for personal choices. This is not so for children, he argues, and consequently opportunities exist for children only in attenuated form. While Howe does not successfully rescue the results standard of measuring opportunities from its conceptual difficulties, he rightly identifies the "outcomes entail choices" criticism as being too picky to warrant an abandonment of such a standard. Also, if we assume that the potential to try hard and to make difficult choices is randomly distributed across racial, class, and gender groups, then comparing the achievement of different groups—as opposed to comparing individuals—should nullify concerns that not lack of opportunities, but lack of effort, is the problem.

Three reminders are helpful before proceeding. First, it is readily apparent that the equal results standard, as formulated by the educationists cited above, is identical to the equal results standard for measuring the degree of general equality of opportunity articulated earlier in the project. Whether it be for the purpose of assessing the degree that equality of occupational opportunity exists in a given society, or for the purpose of assessing the presence of equal educational opportunity specifically, operational concepts such as proportional representation or statistical independence come into play. Regarding educational opportunity and the race variable specifically, is the racial composition in each of the various strata of higher education—elite universities, non-elite four-year universities, and two-year junior colleges—roughly similar to the racial composition in society at large? Or, put another way, are the odds of academic success for any child statistically unrelated to her racial identity? These are the important empirical questions. Second, we must readily acknowledge that the answers to these empirical questions will never be perfect affirmatives. Both the general concept of equal occupational opportunity and its derivative concept of equal educational opportunity imply "a direction of effort, not a goal to be achieved" (quoted earlier, p. 19; Frankel, 1971, p. 209).

Finally, holding equality of educational results across certain social groups as a goal is not the same thing as advocating direct manipulations to bring this about. It is possible to hold equality of results as an institutional ideal and to keep the focus on equalizing opportunities through compensatory programs and school equalization plans, rather than resorting to more manipulative techniques such as radically expanded affirmative action programs at the university level. It cannot be over-emphasized: equal opportunity is the valued ideal; equal results across certain social groups is simply a means of determining its fulfillment.

III. The Story of Equality of Opportunity in Federal Educational Policy

Earliest Manifestations:
The Compensatory Education Thrust
of the 1960s and 1970s

As described above, the Coleman Report and the follow-up studies by Jencks and the Rand Corporation informed Americans that public schools were not as powerful relative to outside educational influences as they traditionally had assumed, and that manipulating traditional input measures such as facilities, curricula, and teacher quality could not be counted on to equalize the disparate academic success-rates of different ethnic and socio-economic groups. It is difficult to demonstrate a direct causal claim between the "schools don't make a difference studies" and the development of major compensatory education programs such as Head Start, Title One, and Upward Bound because two of these programs pre-date the publication of Coleman's study. However, the connection between Coleman's thesis and the justification of new compensatory education efforts is clear. As the name implies, the new compensatory education programs sought to make the overall educational opportunities of children of different social groups more equal by "compensating" for inequalities in children's academic preparation that arise from non-school sources such as families and neighborhoods. Although compensatory education efforts have been overshadowed by the excellence-oriented reforms that are described below, the major programs are still in existence and are the subject of yearly budget debates on the part of policy-makers with different understandings of—or levels of commitment to—equality of educational opportunity.

The First and Second Waves of Excellence-Oriented Reform in the 1980s and Early 1990s

I briefly chronicled in Chapter One the rise of excellence—typically interpreted as higher standards for all students—as the governing ideal for federal educational policy-making since the early 1980s. During the earliest wave of excellence-oriented reform, the idea of raising standards was intertwined with a back-to-the-basics motif. Frustrated by what they perceived as an undemanding, relativistic, individualistic curricular trend throughout the 1970s, many reformers called for longer school-days and school-years, increased instructional time in core subjects like English, Mathematics, and Science, and more frequent tests of students' academic achievement. Or again, as Gretchen Guiton and Jeannie Oakes put it: " 'more of the same' as a way to improve education" (quoted earlier, p. 6; 1995, p. 324).

A more recent wave of excellence-oriented reform, encompassing the late 1980s up until now, is more sophisticated than the first. The emphasis on higher academic standards has remained, but higher-order thinking and problem solving skills have replaced basic skills mastery as the pedagogical targets for all students, both remedial and advanced (Guiton & Oakes,

1995). This phase of education reform began in Charlottesville, Virginia, in 1989, when President Bush met with all of the nation's governors and constructed six National Education Goals toward which all federal and state reform initiatives should point. The fact that a Republican president and all of the nation's governors invested time in developing National Education Goals was quite novel given the American, and quintessentially Republican, tradition of local control of education, not to mention the fact that states bear the constitutional responsibility for public education. The federal government traditionally had limited its role in education to categorical programs for disadvantaged populations, and this was Washington's first move toward involvement in general educational concerns (Jennings, 1995). Still, the defining of national goals was largely symbolic at the time. Bush historically had been a strong advocate of educational decentralization, and it took two more years before he became persuaded to construct voluntary curricular content standards and student performance standards as a way to measure progress toward fulfilling the National Education Goals. He finally did propose content and performance standards in his *America 2000* bill of 1991, which did not become law but did set the parameters for the continuing debate on the federal role in public education.

The Emergence of Opportunity-to-Learn Standards in Federal Education Policy Debates in the Middle 1990s

In response to Bush's *America 2000* proposal, the Congress established a bipartisan National Council on Education Standards and Testing (NCEST), which was charged with studying the feasibility and desirability of national content and performance standards, as well as a corresponding system of assessments to measure students' progress toward meeting these standards. The Council's report, *Raising Standards for Ameri-*

can Education (1992), concluded that a system of voluntary—meaning that states were encouraged, but not required, to follow Washington's lead—national standards and assessment tools was a proper focal point for ongoing education reform (Kildee, 1995). The NCEST's advocacy of content and performance standards was not surprising. The idea of standards-based reform is widespread among academics (Sykes & Plastrik, 1993; Clune, 1993; see Darling-Hammond, 1994, for a dissenting opinion), and, more importantly perhaps, it is supported by most of the major education organizations, business groups, governors, and the current Democratic and former Republican presidents (Jennings, 1995). However, what was surprising was the NCEST's advocacy of a third type of standards alongside content and performance standards: school delivery, or opportunity-to-learn (OTL) standards:

> If national content and performance standards and assessment[s] are not accompanied by clear school delivery standards and policy measures designed to afford all students an equal opportunity to learn...concerns about diminished equity could easily be realized. Standards and assessments must be accompanied by policies that provide access for all students to high quality resources, including appropriate instructional materials and well-prepared teachers. High content and performance standards can be used to challenge all students with the same expectations, but high expectations will only result in common high performance if all schools provide high quality instruction designed to meet the expectations. (NCEST, 1992, p. E12)

According to the NCEST report, OTL standards should be in place before states can properly hold schools and students accountable to high-stakes achievement tests, where schools could face sanctions for school-wide under-performance, and the promotion, graduation, or curricular placement of individual students could be affected by poor performance. Benchmarks need to be established to determine whether or not a school's curriculum, teaching staff, instructional materials, and facilities sufficiently provide all students an authentic chance to meet raised academic expectations (McDonnell, 1995). As Dale E. Kildee (D-Mich.), a former chair of the House of Representatives' Subcommittee on Elementary, Secondary, and Vocational Education and a member of NCEST, put it: "Without delivery standards, you don't know if the school [or larger school system] is failing, or if students are failing" (Rothman, 1993, p. 21).

The NCEST report raised the concept of OTL standards to national attention, and President Bill Clinton's *Goals 2000* proposal in 1994 was obligated to include such standards if it was to gain majority approval in Congress. The original *Goals 2000* framework was modeled after the NCEST report, and it proposed to establish a National Educational Standards and Improvement Council (NESIC) that would establish model content, performance, and OTL standards, and also certify individual state standards for those states that chose to submit them for review. *Goals 2000* defined OTL standards broadly to include: "the criteria for, and the basis of, assessing the sufficiency or quality of the resources, practices, and conditions necessary at each level of the education system (schools, local educational agencies, and States) to provide all students with an opportunity to learn the material in voluntary national content standards or State content standards" (Pub. L. No. 103-227, S. 3 [7]; quoted in McDonnell, 1995, p. 312). More specifically, while Clinton's education bill did not set out OTL standards in detail, it did instruct NESIC to consider the following in developing its model OTL standards:

> (a) the quality and availability to all students of curricula, instructional materials, and technologies...; b) the capability of teachers to provide high-quality instruction to meet diverse learning needs in each content area to all students; c) the extent to which teachers, principals, and administrators have ready and continuing access to professional development...; d) the extent to which curriculum, instructional practices, and

assessments are aligned to voluntary national content standards; e) the extent to which school facilities provide a safe and secure environment for learning and instruction and have the requisite libraries, laboratories, and other resources necessary to provide an opportunity-to-learn; [and] f) the extent to which schools utilize policies, curricula, and instructional practices which ensure non-discrimination on the basis of gender. (108 U.S. Statutes 144; quoted in Dougherty, 1996, p. 41)

The "resources, practices, and conditions" addressed by OTL standards were to be viewed solely through the lense of their effects on classroom instruction, as opposed to the more traditional practice of looking at school inputs—facilities, curricula, and teachers' experience—independently of their utilization in practice. Still, it is significant that the discussion of OTL standards in *Goals 2000* acknowledged the impact of facilities such as classrooms, libraries, and laboratories on students' schooling experiences, rather than minimizing the importance of these capital assets by some sort of claim that these assets—and the money that buys them—are unrelated to children's academic achievement, and thus irrelevant to discussions of equal educational opportunity (McDonnell, 1995; see Hanushek, 1995).

The Political Defeat of Opportunity-to-Learn Standards at the Federal Level

However, the fact that the original version of *Goals 2000* included OTL standards alongside curricular content and student performance standards does not necessarily mean that it treated OTL standards sufficiently. Indeed, the treatment of OTL standards was the major point of contention during congressional deliberations about Clinton's proposal (Guiton & Oakes, 1995; Elmore & Fuhrman, 1995; Porter, 1995; Dougherty, 1996). Liberal Democrats, particularly those on the House of Representatives' Subcommittee on Elementary, Secondary, and

Vocational Education, felt that the Administration's first draft of the bill under-emphasized OTL standards in relation to content and performance standards and pressured Secretary of Education Richard Riley to revise the proposal so that the three types of standards were treated more evenly. These liberal Democrats sought to protect students who, through no fault of their own, attended inferior schools from high-stakes assessments that might negatively affect their educational futures. Riley made some modest adjustments to the bill. As it passed through the House Subcommittee, however, the OTL standards ante was upped considerably. For instance, an amendment was proposed that would require states that adopt the *Goals 2000* agenda, and consequently receive *Goals 2000* funding, to have OTL standards in place before they submit their assessment systems for NESIC approval; this way there could be no window of time in which student achievement would be monitored without proper data concerning the quality of schooling students were experiencing. Another amendment would have required states to prepare to take specific corrective actions if a school or school district did not fulfill the state's OTL standards.

For Republicans on the House Subcommittee, however, these amendments were deal-breakers because they entailed federalist intrusions into states' business (even though states were not required to participate in *Goals 2000* in the first place), as well as a return to a concern with inputs rather than outcomes in federal educational policy-making (Kildee, 1995). At the conclusion of the Subcommittee deliberations, not one Republican voted to forward the amended version of *Goals 2000* to other members of the House. The bill was forwarded anyway, however, because the committee was comprised mainly of Democrats. But then the Democratic advocates of the OTL concept got an unpleasant surprise. President Clinton, anticipating opposition to the bill by Republicans and Southern Democrats in the wider House body and the Senate, sent a letter to the House Subcommittee voicing his disapproval of the proposed amendments, and, for that matter, any further specification of what OTL standards should require of states that receive *Goals 2000* funding. The president wanted to pass an education reform act, and he was willing to soften OTL standards as much as was necessary. Secretary Riley went to work on convincing House Democrats to repeal their amendments, and he was ultimately successful.

The OTL language reflected in the *Goals 2000: Educate America Act,* upon its initial authorization in 1994, was pretty weak (see Guiton & Oakes, 1995; Porter, 1995; McDonnell, 1995). While the law called on states who participated in the program to develop or adopt curricular content and student performance standards and to regularly inform the Department of Education of their progress toward attaining these standards, these states were required only to present "standards *or strategies*" for providing to students sufficient opportunities-to-learn, and the implementation of these strategies was voluntary. Reflecting on Clinton's education bill after its initial authorization, Linda Darling-Hammond summarized the tenuous status of OTL standards in this way: "Although the OTL debate has been raised, it has not succeeded in finding a firm foothold in the *Goals 2000* legislation, where national certification of standards and tests provides teeth for one side of the equation while general exhortations for state and local development of OTL standards provide almost none for the other side—the side that would support children in their learning" (1994, p. 487). Even these weak stipulations, however, did not survive long after initial ratification. In April of 1996, the White House responded to Republican threats on *Goals 2000* budgetary re-authorization— spearheaded by Arlen Specter (R-Pa.), who chairs the Senate appropriations subcommittee that oversees education spending—by allowing all references to OTL standards or strategies to be excised from the legislation. Since 1996, the language of OTL, and by extension the egalitarian sentiment that the concept represents, is completely absent from the Clinton administration's primary educational initiative.

A Brief Explanation of the Defeat of OTL as a Federal Policy Instrument

The demise of OTL as a federal policy vehicle designed to operationalize equality of educational opportunity can be explained at two levels of specificity. It should first be noted that OTL standards are not the only aspect of the *Goals 2000* legislation that have weakened since its inception, and thus the disappearance of OTL terminology cannot be wholly attributed to alleged Republican indifference about equity issues. Even the content and performance standards—the idea of which, at a purely conceptual level, enjoys almost universal support from politicians, business-persons, educators, and parents across the ideological spectrum—have aroused heated criticism, simply because these standards, it is argued, should not be unduly shaped for all children by bureaucrats in Washington, D.C. The idea of the National Education Standards and Improvement Council (NESIC) endorsing model curricular standards and certifying that states have either followed their model or come sufficiently close on their own, simply has not gained acceptance in a nation with a tradition of local control over education and with constitutional responsibility for public education clearly falling on individual states. Even though NESIC likely would have allowed a lot of latitude concerning state-submitted content standards, *Goals 2000* appeared too much like a national curriculum, and pluralist critics such as law professor Stephen Arons (1994) aggressively argued that a national curriculum violates the spirit, if not the letter of the First Amendment. As a result, just like OTL standards, plans to establish NESIC were repealed in April of 1996, and now in order to receive *Goals 2000* funding, states merely have to demonstrate to federal officials that they are in the process of developing content and performance standards, rather than submit their standards for federal certification. In short, the fate of content and performance standards at the federal level has not been much better than that of OTL standards.

However, the downfall of opportunity-to-learn standards at the federal level, unlike its curricular content and student-performance counterparts, is not sufficiently explained by the typically federalist tension between national leadership and individual states' autonomy.[1] Regarding content and performance standards, the requisite political consensus and political will exist; the question is simply who it is that determines these standards. It is now clear to everyone that it will not be the federal government, despite Clinton's earliest, if not fully explicit, hopes for a national curriculum and national assessments to match. Debates already are raging in individual states about this very issue of centralization of curricular decision-making power versus decentralized power located in local communities, and, constitutionally speaking, this is where the debate should be. Opportunity-to-learn standards, on the other hand, have not gained sufficient political consensus or political will. Concerning political consensus, the task of operationalizing the concept was only in its nascent stages; scholars such as Andrew Porter (1995), Lorraine M. McDonnell (1995), and Richard Elmore and Susan Fuhrman (1995) went a long way toward clarifying the policy implications of OTL, but the policy-making community had not come very far itself. Consequently, the relatively undefined nature of OTL's policy implications exacerbated the federalist problem it shared with the *Goals 2000* legislation as a whole. The political fate of OTL standards also was determined by a failure of will, although this phenomenon was less conspicuous than that of gaining consensus. Even if politicians had been able to agree upon the logical importance of instituting OTL standards to ensure that disadvantaged children were not unfairly harmed by high-stakes tests associated with new content and performance standards, OTL was more problematic than its content and performance counterparts. Whatever the operationally complex concept meant in practice, it sounded much more expensive to policy-makers than deciding what children should know and designing some tests to figure out if they had learned it. It was easy prey for partisan politics, and as a result, the OTL-related requirements for states to receive federal funding were not just softened, as were content and performance standards, but rather the language of OTL was eliminated completely.

IV. The Status
of Equal Educational Opportunity
in State-Level Educational Policy

Attention to Opportunity-to-Learn
and Equity Issues at the State Level

Although the architects of *Goals 2000* no longer can point to any universally acknowledged accountability procedure such as NESIC review of states' proposed content and performance standards, every one of the fifty individual states have availed themselves of *Goals 2000* funding by designing specific learning targets and corresponding assessment tools for K-12 students. But, the relevant question for this project is: How is the opportunity-to-learn construct—which was envisioned as an equity check against the introduction of high-stakes assessments by Clinton's Education Department and certain House Democrats—faring at the state level? The fact that it was eliminated from federal legislation due to partisan politics does not necessarily entail that the concept would not be alive and kicking in several or more state-houses. Sadly, the surprising reality is that the OTL concept has received only sporadic popular or scholarly attention since its disappearance from the federal scene in 1996.

If one surveys the last two years of *Education Week,* one finds scant reference to OTL standards. A search of the Educational Resources Information Center (ERIC) database reveals a similar paucity of recent scholarly attention to the concept since Porter's, McDonnell's, and Elmore and Fuhrman's pioneering research in 1995. While surprising, the reason behind the term's fall from favor is not unusual in the domain of political policy-making. Simply put, OTL was the most politicized aspect of early *Goals 2000* negotiation between the two dominant parties, and the eventual Republican victory in Washington, D.C., was so complete as to mark the term "opportunity-to-learn"—as distinct from the policy concerns it represented—as a political loser. For instance, when Karen Diegmueller and Millicent Lawton of *Education Week* covered a major education policy summit in New York just one month after the Republicans had all of the OTL references erased from *Goals 2000,* they noted that many conferees voiced OTL-type issues, but abstained for strategic reasons from using the politically damaged term (May 29, 1996).

Students of politics understand that while policy terms such as OTL appear less frequently after they sustain political damage, the moral and political ideals they were intended to operationalize typically re-emerge in the American political dialectic, albeit with new, "fresh" terminology. Recall from the discussion above that OTL itself was a re-packaging of "school delivery standards," a term which connotes similar concerns with the quality of input variables such as instructional facilities, curriculum materials, teaching personnel, and technology, although it is true that OTL advocates only referenced these variables in relation to their effect on student-learning outcomes, and never as ends in themselves. John F. Jennings (1997), an educational policy analyst based in Washington, D.C., understands the equity implications of neglecting OTL concerns while proceeding with standards-based reform, and he recently surveyed three major studies of standards-based school reform in the fifty states—all published in 1997—in order to see whether or not equity concerns were being addressed alongside curricular-content and student-performance issues. Jennings knew that while in some states he would find explicit reference to OTL standards or strategies, in other states he might find evidence of OTL-related efforts that simply were not named as such, given the questionable political status of the OTL term. Consequently, his search is best described as an assessment of the degree to which individual states are addressing broad equity issues that arise in relation to their experiments with raising academic standards and attaching high stakes tests to them—tests which impact students' grade promotion or graduation, or which possibly lead to the withdrawal of resources from already impoverished schools. The findings of the three recent studies of standards-based reform in the states that Jennings refers to are briefly summarized below.

According to "Making Standards Matter" (1997), the American Federation of Teachers' (AFT) last installment in a recently established series of annual reports on states' efforts to design and implement academic standards, only thirteen states are identified as making even minimal efforts to design and fund intervention programs for students who fail to make the mark: Arkansas, Florida, Illinois, Indiana, Kentucky, Lousiana, Minnesota, Nevada, New York, North Carolina, Ohio, South Carolina, and Texas. "The rest of the states," the authors conclude, "seem to be assuming the problem will take care of itself" (internet, 1997). The Council of Chief State School Officers' 1997 report on states' progress regarding Mathematics and Science standards design and implementation is helpful because agreement on content and performance standards in these curricular areas has come much more quickly than in the more politically contentious areas of Social Studies and English. While one might hope that the relative ease of identifying learning targets in Mathematics and Science would have freed up time for educators in these areas to address OTL issues with greater specificity, the council's study concludes the contrary:

> Two major shortcomings were found by our review panel. First, the standards typically outline a comparable curriculum for all students moving through K-12, but the panel did not find good examples of a vision of how current school curriculum and school organization will need to change to reach this goal. Second, with a few exceptions, the review panel does not see standards or criteria that would provide a way to evaluate whether any equity goal had been accomplished. (p. 18)

"Persistence and Change: Standards-Based Systemic Reform in Nine States" (1997), a policy brief published by the Consortium for Policy Research in Education (CPRE), which monitors reform efforts in California, Connecticut, Florida, Georgia, Kentucky, Minnesota, New Jersey, South Carolina, and Texas, reports similar discoveries: "For the most part, attention to equity issues within the context of standards-based reform remained episodic and weak." Concerning opportunity-to-learn standards specifically, the authors conclude that "in most of our states, as in most of the nation, opportunity-to-learn standards specifying the various learning conditions to which all students should have access were not on the policy agenda" (p. 9; see also Council of Chief State School Officers, 1995).

An Exceptional Case: Steps Toward Substantive Equal Educational Opportunity in New Jersey

As these studies indicate, the consensus opinion is that the standards and assessment movement in the states—the excellence movement—has not been accompanied by serious and persistent efforts to incorporate equity concerns into reform plans. Equity issues continue to surround school finance and desegregation policies, but there has been very little integration between equity efforts in these areas and *Goals 2000* standards-based reform (CPRE, 1997). The CPRE study, however, does cite New Jersey, which "openly embraced opportunity-to-learn standards as part of a strategic plan to bundle equity, a long-running dispute over school funding, and standards," as one exception (p. 9). Like fourteen other states across the nation (see Hickrod et al., 1997), the New Jersey legislature's recent attention to equity issues has been mandated by the state Supreme Court. The most recent ruling in May of 1998 solidifies the precedent set by four previous rulings requiring equalization of financial resources across rich and poor school districts, which in New Jersey's case correspond with the most dramatic disparities between urban and suburban wealth-bases in the United States.

The political dialogue preceding the New Jersey Supreme Court decision, which the justices described as "the last major judicial involvement in the long and tortuous history of the state's extraordinary effort to bring a thorough and efficient education to the children in its poorest school districts" (Hendrie, 1998, internet), is relevant to our concerns here. Christine Todd Whitman, the Republican Governor, and the GOP-dominated legislature attempted to reframe the conversation about financial equity, shifting it from a focus on equality of per-pupil spending to a focus on what financial resources were minimally necessary to ensure that any given child in one of the Abbott districts experienced an education sufficiently "thorough and efficient" to successfully meet the state's new curriculum standards.[2] While critics at the Newark-based Education Law Center, the legal representatives of the Abbott districts, charged that Whitman's standards proposal was "a sham" (Harp, 1996), a mere decoy to take the attention off per-pupil spending equity, the Supreme Court partially disagreed. In a unanimous decision handed down in April of 1998, New Jersey's high court affirmed the logic of locating school finance policies within the broader context of standards-based reform, but it also upheld previous rulings requiring per-pupil spending equity between poor urban and wealthy suburban districts. This decision is important because it successfully negotiated the tension between an out-comes-based interpretation of the state's obligation to provide all children with a sufficient opportunity to learn—as measured by their ability to meet rigorous curriculum standards—and one strict input variable that is necessary for the standards movement to have at least minimal credibility: parity of per-pupil spending across rich and poor school districts.

The New Jersey Supreme Court decision represents a significant step toward realizing formal equality of educational opportunity, which is no small achievement. Following a steadily emerging legal precedent across the nation, the high court recognized that the principle of non-discrimination entails more than simple access to free, common schools: it entails access to schools that are funded at a level commensurate with other schools in the state. More relevant to our purposes here, however, the recent New Jersey ruling actually moves past the formal conception of equality of educational opportunity toward the substantive conception advanced in this project. The written opinion in the New Jersey case not only requires that the Abbott districts spend as much per-pupil as wealthier districts, but also makes it clear that the Abbott districts should spend even more. Actually, the high court reversed a lower-court decision that prescribed costly new compensatory programs in urban districts, such as full-day pre-school programs for three and four year-olds. However, the reasoning behind this decision was not that such programs were unnecessary, but that the plans for additional compensatory programs should come from the bottom up, with opportunity-to-learn strategies and corresponding programs developed at the district level and not prescribed by the courts. Again, the Supreme Court justices wrote that they fully expected that more would be spent per-pupil in urban than in suburban districts if the state were truly as committed to helping poor students meet rigorous standards as it professed to be (Hendrie, 1998).

One potential rebuttal should be recognized before proceeding. Recall from the previous chapter that the substantive conception of equal opportunity is not perfectly compatible with the formal conception. In this respect, formalists might protest that New Jersey's move toward substantive equality of educational opportunity is actually unjust. Taken literally, the principle of non-discrimination entailed by the formal conception requires that there be no funding disparities between rich and poor school districts, and that includes differences that favor the poor. However, assuming that the moral superiority of the substantive conception over the formal conception was successfully demonstrated in Chapter Three, this conflict in practice should be recognized, but requires no apologies. Robert E. Slavin's (1994) description of what economists call "overburden" in the Baltimore City schools provides a useful rationale for disproportionate educational spending on behalf of poor districts. According to Slavin, Baltimore City spends almost twenty-three percent of its school funds on Special Education, as opposed to fourteen percent state-wide, and the beleaguered district employs more school security guards than there are police officers in the majority of Maryland counties. Consequently, the proportion of the Baltimore City budget that is devoted to regular instruction is smaller than any other jurisdiction. Moreover, Slavin anticipates the conservative retort that Baltimore City's budget problems arise from a bloated administrative staff; Baltimore City spends less than the state average on administration, and if the central office were shut down completely and devoted to regular instruction, the district would only rise from last place in per-pupil regular instruction costs to third from last. Finally, Slavin observes that the Maryland case is not at all atypical in regard to public school financing in the United States.

V. The Potential of Opportunity-to-Learn Standards For Operationalizing Equal Educational Opportunity

The Transformation of OTL
from a Technical to a Normative Concept

One of the ways that scholarly research serves public policy-makers is by providing them with concepts that allow them to express, implement, and measure progress on the goals that they value (McDonnell, 1995). Lorraine M. McDonnell describes concepts that enable policy-makers to operationalize their moral and political commitments as "generative concepts": "A generative concept...not only captures the normative assumptions embodied in a particular policy goal, but also synthesizes empirical data so as to identify a particular strategy for achieving the goal, and perhaps even provides a guide for how to measure progress in moving toward the goal" (p. 304). According to McDonnell, OTL is just such a concept. The concept of OTL was first employed three decades ago during cross-national comparisons of students' mathematical achievement carried out by the International Association for the Evaluation of Educational Achievement (IEA). IEA researchers recognized that, when comparing the mathematical achievement of students from different countries, it was technically important to account for differences in curricular opportunities that might impact the way particular students performed on IEA assessments. Hence, they developed the concept of opportunity-to-learn to help them control for differences in curricular exposure across countries. The OTL concept quietly influenced the development of large-scale educational indicators in the middle-1980s, but it was its emergence in the recent policy debates on standards-based reform that first brought it to public attention.

In the midst of accelerating standards-based reform in the early and middle-1990s, liberal scholars and politicians discovered a different purpose for the OTL concept. OTL standards could be used to hold state school systems responsible for ensuring that individual schools had the resources they needed to provide each child with an ample opportunity to meet new performance standards, especially when failure to meet such standards triggered undesirable consequences for both students and schools. Now, it is important to note the shift in the way that OTL standards were understood and employed; a purely technical function gave way to a moral and philosophical function, although this moral function was complemented by the capacity of the concept to provide cohesiveness to empirical concerns as well. In McDonnell's own words:

> Although implicit in the IEA researchers' conceptualization of OTL was a belief that students should not be assessed on knowledge that they had not been given an opportunity to learn, their main concern was ensuring the technical validity of their findings. It was only when OTL entered the policy arena that normative assumptions about a social contract and the nature of equal educational opportunity became dominant. Yet it was these normative assumptions, combined with a compelling set of empirical findings about the relationship between students' curricular exposure and their achievement, that propelled OTL from the relative obscurity of research publications to a topic of Congressional debate. (p. 306)

As a generative concept, OTL does possess great potential to help policy-makers and educators operationalize their normative convictions about equality of educational opportunity. However, even before it sustained political damage, the conceptualization of OTL as a policy instrument was only at the "emerging idea stage" (Porter, 1995, p. 21), and its compatibility with the substantive vision of equal educational opportunity advanced here will depend on how its definition evolves.

*The Move to Define OTL in Terms of Outcomes
Rather Than Inputs and Processes*

In section two above, I recounted the evolution of the concept of equality of educational opportunity from one that was primarily concerned with school-related input and process variables to one that is primarily concerned with the outputs of schooling—meaning the actual effects of input and process variables in terms of students' academic achievement. The prime movers behind this redefinition—James Coleman, and later Thomas Green, Kenneth Strike, and Kenneth Howe, among others—did not mean to discount the importance of input and process standards, but simply wanted to remind policy-makers that these standards were merely the means required to accomplish a larger purpose: authentic equality of opportunity as measured by increasing parity of achievement across racial and socioeconomic groups. For Coleman and his followers, federal and state-initiated input and process variables such as financial equalization policies or compensatory programs for disadvantaged students were not ends in themselves—the provision of which fulfilled the state's educational obligations—but were simply tools. Elmore and Fuhrman (1995), writing almost thirty years after Coleman first introduced an outcomes-based conception of equal educational opportunity, re-articulate his emphasis on results. Elmore and Fuhrman argue that states have overused input and process standards in the past, indulging a "culture of regulation" that has established layer upon layer of input and process requirements without proper regard to their collective coherence or to their empirical utility in terms of closing the educational achievement gap between certain groups (p. 438). In their words:

> As we enter the twenty-first century, the definition of equal opportunity is expanding beyond the prior definitions that

have driven state policy efforts. No longer is equal access to essential services or compensatory efforts seen as sufficient. With the development of state content and performance standards, policy-makers have shifted the focus of their equity concern to outcomes. The standards movement suggests that all children should have an equal chance to meet challenging outcome expectations, and they should receive instruction to prepare them to meet these outcomes. Assuring that essential services and the resources that fund them are comparable across districts and schools is no longer enough.

Now, standards policies are designed to assure that schools and districts use resources and provide services effectively for students. Schools are expected to provide, and states are expected to guarantee, not just course offerings but high-quality curricula that support the content and performance standards, and not just certified teachers but teachers who are well prepared to teach the material in the standards. In this latest phase, opportunity-to-learn means providing all students in society equal opportunity to reach ambitious outcomes, and that implies that schools must not only have resources but use them well so that quality instruction results. (p. 438)

The Continuing Need for a Minimum Core of Input and Process Standards

Elmore and Fuhrman are correct about the bulkiness and lack of coherence characterizing most states' policy packages related to equality of educational opportunity. Respect for educators as professionals requires that they be granted a significant degree of latitude in determining what programs will best serve their students, particularly those students at greatest risk of academic failure. However, Elmore and Fuhrman also recognize that just because input and process standards have been thoughtlessly layered upon one another—new regulations arriving, but no regulations leaving—it does not mean that a coherent "minimum core" of input and process standards is unnecessary

(p. 452). Clearly, establishing input and process standards does not fulfill a state's equal educational opportunity obligations independently of the actual effectiveness of these standards for equalizing educational achievement across racial and socio-economic groups. However, it is equally obvious that while input and process standards are means and not ends in themselves, they are essential means. Equality of educational outcomes across certain social groups cannot occur without at least some input and process standards; the real debate concerns how aggressively this minimum core of standards is defined.

A Case in Point:
The Need For Equalizing Per-Pupil Spending
Across Rich and Poor School Districts

My critique of Elmore and Fuhrman's argument is that they are not sufficiently explicit about what a minimum core of input and process regulations must necessarily include. Consider the most basic, and most politicized, of input variables: annual per-pupil expenditures. Surely the debate about whether the problems of urban school districts can be solved by increased funding will continue (see Hanushek, 1995), but the balance of opinion holds that money indeed matters. Moreover, unlike other input and process regulations such as those concerning students' hours-per-week in school, the number of core courses required to graduate, or mandatory pull-out programs associated with Chapter One funds, it is difficult to make the case that simply providing financial resources to individual school districts violates the professional prerogative of local educators to make their own pedagogical decisions. Thus, unlike many other input and process variables, there is no real strategic reason why per-pupil spending should not be equalized across rich and poor districts. Yet, despite recent legal victories in New Jersey and several other states requiring more equitable school funding as a fulfillment of these states' constitutional responsibility to provide equal educational opportunity, the United States remains the only country in the world to allow elementary and secondary education funding to be in part determined by local wealth (Slavin, 1994). While Elmore and Fuhrman are correct that a lack of strategic consistency is a major factor in the states' failures to secure equality of educational opportunity across racial and socio-economic groups, the conspicuous absence of equality of spending per-pupil in many states arises from a different shortcoming: a failure of moral and political will.

Although Elmore and Fuhrman do cite political dysfunction—where legislators seek only to appease their own constituencies in order to prolong their stay in office, as opposed to following their consciences—as one of several causes of states' problems with providing equal educational opportunity, they do not give it the emphasis it deserves. Several other writers, on the other hand, see the moral and political problem more clearly. Regarding school funding inequalities as discussed above (see Taylor & Piche, 1990; Barton, Coley, & Goertz, 1991; Kozol, 1991; Massell & Fuhrman, 1993), Slavin states that "the system that determines education funding for most American elementary and secondary students is a national disgrace" (1994, p. 98). Peter Cookson Jr. calls the over-crowded, dilapidated schools in inner cities "a national scandal and an affront to a basic sense of decency" (1995, p. 415). Yet, the most famous—or perhaps infamous—critic of the American system of school funding is Jonathan Kozol, whose book *Savage Inequalities* (1991) is about this very problem. Speaking of funding inequities in the state of California, which represent the norm in America and not the exception, Kozol writes:

> The consequence [of unequal funding] is easily discerned by visitors. Beverly Hills still operates a high school that, in academic excellence, can rival those of Princeton and Winnetka. Baldwin Park still operates a poorly funded and inferior

system. In Northern California, Oakland remains a mainly nonwhite, poor and troubled system while the schools that serve the Piedmont district, separately incorporated though it is surrounded on four sides by Oakland, remains richly funded, white, and excellent. The range of district funding in the state is still extremely large: The poorest districts spend less than $3,000 [per-pupil] while the wealthiest spend more than $7,000...

The lesson of California is that equity in education represents a formidable threat to other values held by many affluent Americans...[values that are] profoundly rooted in American ideas about the right and moral worth of individual advancement at whatever cost to others who may be less favored by the accident of birth...

There is deep seated reverence for fair play in the United States, and in many areas of life we see the consequences in a genuine distaste for loaded dice; but this is not the case in education, health care, or inheritance of wealth. In these elemental areas we want the game to be unfair and we have made it so; and it will likely so remain. (pp. 221-223)

VI. Conclusion:
Input and Process Standards and the Alleviation of Educational Disadvantagement

In the discussion above, I described how Americans' historic and naive faith in the ability of their public schools—operating in a traditional manner—to equalize life prospects for children born into different social conditions was shaken in the 1960s and early 1970s. In response to this realization, Coleman and several educational philosophers who followed him have re-articulated in explicit, measurable terms what Mann meant when he referred to our common schools as the "great equalizer." Federal and state-level policy-makers initially sought to operationalize this vision by establishing a variety of compensatory education programs. However, while many of these compensatory programs still exist, more recent political debates about equal educational opportunity have centered around the inclusion of opportunity-to-learn standards, or some more generic attention to input and process standards, alongside curricular content and student performance standards as part of current outcome-based school reform efforts. OTL standards have not yet gained a firm foothold in educational politics, but it is my conviction that this concept has great potential as a centerpiece for future deliberations about the policy implications of substantive equality of educational opportunity. The social and political complexities surrounding the definition of OTL standards are significant, but recent policy history demonstrates a continuing need to attend to input and process concerns in order to proclaim higher standards for all with any degree of credulity.

As a segue to the final chapter, I want to connect the discussion of input and process standards—which I will continue to call OTL standards, despite the tenuous political status of the term—to my explanations for educational disadvantagement in Chapter Two. I argued above that equalizing per-pupil expenditures between wealthy and poor districts, or even tilting the scale in the favor of poor districts, is an important place to start. Although some might object (see Hanushek, 1995), I will assume that money has the potential to make a difference for disadvantaged students, and concentrate on the more interesting question: Money spent on what? We have known since Coleman's study in the 1960s that improvements in macro-variables such as instructional facilities, curriculum materials, and teacher pay, while important, are insufficient in themselves to close the achievement gap between mainstream and non-mainstream students. In the following chapter, I will make some recommendations about how we might employ increased resources in ways that do make a difference for disadvantaged students. My remarks will address both social inequalities that are beyond schools and problems within schooling itself that contribute to the disproportionate failure rates of racial and ethnic-minority and poor students. I will be careful to make these recommendations cohere with my previous explanations of educational disadvantagement; the solutions need to match the problems.

Notes

1. The term "federalism" is often mistakenly understood as connoting centralized power in the hands of a national government, but its true meaning refers to the interplay between local initiative and centralized authority. In the context of the United States, federalism refers to a policy orientation that seeks a proper balance between states' rights and national interests.
2. The term "Abbott districts" refers to 28 poor, urban districts that have been associated with the *Abbott v. Burke* case, which has been continuously litigated since 1981.

Chapter Five

Conclusion:
Broad Policy Recommendations
and Final Philosophical Exhortations

I. A Summary of the Arguments
Presented Thus Far

While I have aimed throughout this project to present a consistent and coherent vision of the role that K-12 education might play in securing distributive justice in a given society—anchoring this vision in what I have called a substantive interpretation of equality of educational and occupational opportunity (see also O'Neill, 1977; Galston, 1986)—the approach taken has been multi-disciplinary and the resulting product is multi-layered. The book is most easily summarized by reviewing the individual chapters. The main purpose of the introductory chapter was to demonstrate the practical importance of revisiting the moral ideal of equal educational opportunity. I pointed to the paucity and superficiality of attention the ideal has received in the major school reform documents that have framed the educational excellence movement since the early 1980s, which contrasts markedly with the sustained emphasis on equalizing opportunities that characterized the previous two decades.

I have described the middle three chapters as sociological, philosophical, and political in approach. In the sociological chapter, I identified what kinds of children would be the main beneficiaries of a renewed effort to equalize educational opportunities, explaining the processes by which social background characteristics such as racial identity and socio-economic status impact children's academic success through mediating variables that sociologists of schooling refer to as cultural and educational "capital." In the philosophical chapter, I presented the normative core of the project, which is the claim that the substantive interpretation of equality of opportunity—and equal educational opportunity by extension—is morally superior to the formal interpretation. The substantive interpretation of equality of opportunity sets as its ultimate, if not perfectly attainable goal the realization of an authentic meritocracy, where the life chances of any given generation of individual children depend solely upon their initiative and ability, and not upon morally irrelevant characteristics such as the economic success of their parents, the color of their skin, or their gender. In the politics chapter, I chronicled the fate of a policy vehicle called opportunity-to-learn standards at the federal and state levels, and expressed my conviction that debates concerning the definition of OTL standards have opened up a critical space in which to locate a moral argument for substantive equality of educational opportunity.

In this final chapter, I will accomplish three tasks. I will first offer some broad strategies that policy-makers might follow in order to equalize children's educational opportunities in the substantive sense advanced here. Having made these recommendations, I will then return to philosophical discourse and attempt to persuade readers that substantive equality of opportunity, or authentic meritocracy, coheres with our deepest intuitions concerning the equitable organization of societies, or at least one important aspect of the arrangement of societies. Finally, I will conclude the project by returning to where I started: the task of negotiating between educational excellence and equality of opportunity, two ideals that are self-evidently desirable, but which exist in chronic tension with one another in educational practice.

II. Recommendations for Implementing Substantive Equality of Educational Opportunity

The Continuing Appeal of Opportunity-to-Learn Standards

As articulated in Chapter Four, Lorraine M. McDonnell (1995) describes OTL as a new generative concept that possesses unique potential to mobilize educational policy-making in two ways. First, it helps us translate our normative commitments to the social contract and equality of educational opportunity into policy language, or at least it provides a centering concept around which we can clarify our normative disagreements. Second, it can serve as an umbrella term that encompasses an emerging set of empirical findings about what constitutes an adequate opportunity for all students to learn the material that we expect schools to teach. It provides a space in which to locate this critical question (after which a whole set of sub-questions would follow): What combination of school resources (inputs) and teaching practices (processes) will most effectively realize scholastic achievement for all students, especially those students who possess characteristics correlated with chronic educational failure? This is the very same question I would pose concerning the implementation of substantive equality of educational opportunity. Consequently, despite the tenuous political status of the OTL concept, I continue to be intrigued by its potential and will center my recommendations for implementing substantive equality of educational opportunity around it.

An Exhortatory and a Regulatory Function for OTL Standards

I believe that the future utility of OTL standards will depend upon how they are employed. Recall that the original *Goals 2000* legislation required states to include OTL "standards or strategies" in their annual improvement plans in order to receive funding awards, but there was no follow-up mechanism to see if they took these standards or strategies seriously. Two years later, the OTL stipulations were eliminated completely. Unfortunately, the prevailing attitude is one of resistance to federal input and process stipulations, and it is politically difficult to attach such stipulations to a funding program in which every state participates. However, since states' participation in *Goals 2000* is voluntary, it cannot be assumed that federally-initiated OTL standards violate states' constitutional authority over public education. Attaching OTL standards to federal assistance is different than regulating states' educational efforts without their consent. The original *Goals 2000* vision was exhortatory, not regulatory. I think that the National Education Standards and Improvement Council (NESIC), one charge of which was to certify individual state's OTL standards as well as their content and performance standards, should be re-established. If individual states do not wish to adopt OTL standards, or choose to define them more loosely than NESIC would wish, they do not have to participate in the program. If President Bill Clinton had chosen this strategy, he could have truly set an equitable agenda for public education and honored our constitutional tradition of state autonomy in educational matters at the same time.

If the Department of Education were to re-establish NESIC and design a set of OTL standards with some regulatory "teeth," as Linda Darling-Hammond puts it (1994, p. 487), it is quite possible that many states would respond. But the obstacles are great. Implementing OTL standards at the state level would be expensive because many communities lack the fiscal and administrative resources to meet them, and in order to subsidize the efforts of poor districts states would have to increase the taxes laid upon the wealthy. Also, making OTL commitments explicit would exacerbate state governments' vulnerability to lawsuits levied on behalf of poor districts. Although these kinds of lawsuits are occurring anyway (see Hickrod et al., 1997), most state officials do not wish to make the plaintiffs' cases any easier by putting any OTL commitments in print (McDonnell, 1995). However, while these political constraints might be powerful, they are worth the risk. As argued in Chapter Three, the liberal ideal of the equal moral worth of persons is best respected by economic policies that equalize as much as possible the life chances—the positive liberty—of each generation of children. I submit that the states' moral and constitutional responsibility to provide equality of educational opportunity overrides any problems that will arise in the process.

Five Recommendations
for the Future Development of OTL Standards

I will now construct a vision of good practice that takes the broad OTL recommendations in the original *Goals 2000* legislation as its starting point, and then fills in some gaps. I will not repeat my previous arguments for school funding equity—or disproportionate spending on behalf of poor districts—but will assume that increased funding provides the resources with which poor districts can improve their services and that the more interesting questions concern how such dollars are most effectively spent. Recall that the original *Goals 2000* legislation recommended that NESIC consider the following in developing more specific OTL standards:

> (a) the quality and availability to all students of curricula, instructional materials, and technologies...; (b) the capability

of teachers to provide high-quality instruction to meet diverse learning needs in each content area to all students; (c) the extent to which teachers, principals, and administrators have ready and continuing access to professional development...; (d) the extent to which curriculum, instructional practices, and assessments are aligned to voluntary national content standards; (e) the extent to which school facilities provide a safe and secure environment for learning and instruction and have the requisite libraries, laboratories, and other resources necessary to provide an opportunity-to-learn; [and] (f) the extent to which schools utilize policies, curricula, and instructional practices which ensure non-discrimination on the basis of gender. (quoted earlier, p. 122; 108 U.S. Statutes 144; quoted in Dougherty, 1996, p. 41)

The investments in physical capital items called for in items *a* and *e* of *Goals 2000's* OTL guidelines are inarguably important. The dilapidated conditions of facilities, worn-out instructional materials, and out-dated technology in many poor districts has been widely recognized since James Bryant Conant's 1961 book, *Slums and Suburbs* (see Kozol, 1991, for more recent descriptions). However, my first four recommendations will focus on items *b* and *c*, which address teaching and learning specifically (*b* and *c* impact *d* and *f*, in turn). I do this because I want my proposed solutions to match my diagnosis of the problems in Chapter Two, one part of which centers around culturally-influenced interactions between middle-class teachers and non-mainstream students that often result in low expectations of these students and their disproportionate placement in low-ability groups.[1] Since the time of the Coleman Report, scholars have understood that differences between schools on crude macro-variables such as the quality of facilities and curricular materials do not adequately explain what happens in classrooms that results in educational inequality, nor can they help us see what should be done to make things better (see Mehan, 1992). I believe that improving the teaching and learning process itself is the key to successful education reform. In the words of George F. Madaus, himself borrowing from Parker J. Palmer: "Teachers...must be the cornerstone of any systemic reform directed at improving our schools.... [Policy-makers] have lost sight of the fact that...'the teacher is a mediator between the knower and the known, between the learner and the learned'" (quoted in Darling-Hammond, 1994, p. 482).

Recommendation One: Produce Teachers Who Are Multiculturally Literate

If the quality of teacher-student interactions in instructional settings is, as Geneva Gay (1997) says, "the ultimate test of educational quality" (p. 223), then the preparation and continued professional development of teachers is of paramount importance for raising the academic performance of non-mainstream students. More specifically, Gay understands the cultural incongruity that many non-mainstream students experience in school— as described in Chapter Two—and recommends that America's teaching force be educated or re-educated so that they can deliver "culturally responsive" instruction to these students (p. 224). For Gay, this re-education should have four main emphases. First, she calls on teacher-training institutions to increase their charges' awareness about their own cultural identities— their assumptions, values, and communication styles—and to realize that their identities might predispose them to underestimate the abilities of students from different cultural backgrounds. Second, she encourages teachers and prospective teachers to actively study the assumptions, values, and communication styles of the student populations they encounter in their classrooms, or expect to encounter in the near future. Third, teachers should study the different learning styles that are cultivated in non-mainstream cultures and how they might teach in ways that complement such styles, although there are great person-to-person variations within any particular culture. Finally, Gay advises that teachers become more proficient at public relations, particularly in regard to communicating with non-mainstream parents, whose cooperation is essential if their children are to thrive in the classroom.

In order to substantiate a recommendation that teachers become more multiculturally literate, it is important to provide evidence that such an approach would increase the academic achievement levels of non-mainstream students. This apparently has not been easy. Proponents of multicultural education have successfully argued that culturally responsive curriculum and instruction is imperative for any diverse society that aspires to democracy (see Gay, 1997; Campbell, 1996; Singer, 1992), but they have produced little empirical data concerning its effect on student-learning, at least as measured by standardized measures of academic achievement. One significant and encouraging exception to this gap in the literature is the longitudinal data from KEEP, the Kamehameha Early Education Project directed by Roland G. Tharp and his colleagues. Throughout the 1970s and early 1980s, participating private and public elementary-school teachers learned how to teach in ways that were more compatible with the cultural backgrounds of native Hawaiian and Navajo children in Hawaii, California, and Arizona, focusing on just those aspects of instruction that were identified as problematic for non-mainstream populations in Chapter Two. For example, KEEP-trained teachers emphasized small-group activities over lecture methods for native Hawaiian children who come from kinship-oriented cultures that value collaboration among children and their collective independence from adult guidance. When they led discussions with Native Hawaiian children, they de-emphasized solitary turn-taking in favor of a more informal style where students felt free to interact, interrupt, and construct responses together. When working on reading comprehension with Navajo children, they quit dissecting stories and postponed discussion of them until the conclusion, in keeping with the Navajo tradition of story-telling and consistent with what they believe is a holistic versus an analytical learning style (see Chapter Two; Tharp, 1982, 1989). KEEP researchers discovered that the needs of native Hawaiian and Navajo children differed in some cases and called for different instructional strategies, but one consistent theme emerged. When teaching materials drew upon children's background knowledge and when teachers taught in ways that were familiar to them, both student populations prospered.

Internal (Tharp, 1982) and external (Calfee et al., 1981) evaluators have confirmed KEEP's effectiveness in terms of increasing non-mainstream students' reading skills in both private and public schools. Surely, reading is only one academic skill, but it is perhaps the most crucial one. What is especially encouraging is that the gains made by KEEP students in relation to their peers were stable over time. Even with substantial implementation problems in the early years and persistently high rates of student and teacher transience, a ten-year study of 3,345 children demonstrated a statistically significant relationship between years of participation in the program and academic achievement (Klein, 1988). However, after nearly two decades of significant private and public monetary investment in the KEEP experiment with culturally responsive instruction, a new generation of administrators in the Hawaii state department have determined that the program is too costly, a development which Tharp and his colleagues view as an unfortunate reflection of how hard it is to build the capacity for change into public education systems (Tharp & Gallimore, 1988). As L. Scott Miller (1995) notes, this resistance to change is especially regrettable given the fact that the proportion of non-white students in America's schools has increased dramatically in recent years and will continue to increase unabated. But Tharp and his colleagues continue to work, and, critical to our purposes here, have developed a teacher-training program (Pre-Service Education for Teachers of Minorities, or PETOM) at the University of Hawaii that will complement their KEEP efforts (Dalton, Tharp, & Blaine, 1987). This is the kind of attention to the preparation of multiculturally literate teachers that Gay recommends. The two decades of effort by Sharp and his colleagues have demonstrated that such an endeavor can be fruitful, not just for the self-esteem or happiness of non-mainstream students, but for their academic success as well.[2]

Recommendation Two: Re-Assess Ability Grouping and Tracking Practices

Another problem described in Chapter Two that effects teaching and learning in K-12 classrooms is the common practice of ability grouping, or tracking, as it is called at the secondary level. The researchers and educators who understand the problems that ability grouping causes for non-mainstream students can be placed in two broad categories: moderates who believe that ability grouping makes basic educational sense provided that certain restraints exist, and "radicals" who advocate the complete abolition of ability grouping, an approach that is often referred to as "de-tracking." The constraints that the moderates would place on ability-grouping practices are as follows: (1) ability grouping only should occur in a few subjects like English and Mathematics; (2) the smaller number of groups, and the more heterogeneous they are, the better; (3) the same material should be covered in all groups so that all students have access to high-priority knowledge, even if the pace and depth of exposure vary; (4) mobility between groups should be as fluid as possible, so that students are never "stuck" in a group that does not fit them; and (5) in the case of between-class grouping or tracking (rather than within-class grouping), the number of students in the higher groups should be as large as possible relative to the number of students in lower groups. For instance, it would be fine if 60 percent of high school sophomores were in a college-preparatory track; and (6) make sure that teachers working with the lower groups are excellent, rather than simply the ones who did not "earn" the privilege of teaching the high-achievers (recommendations 1-3 are from Braddock & McPartland, 1990; 4-5 are from Gamoran, 1992; recommendation 6 is from Hallinan, 1994; cited in Dougherty, 1996).

The more aggressive advocates of de-tracking believe that teachers can be trained to provide stimulating instruction to students of all ability levels in heterogeneous classrooms, although they acknowledge that a great deal of new research and training will be required to implement this reform on a wide scale (Oakes, 1992, 1994, 1995; Oakes & Lipton, 1992; Wheelock, 1992). Proponents of heterogeneous grouping also understand that they face an uphill battle because the assumptions that undergird ability-grouping practices run very deep in the American psyche. Many educators still believe that human intelligence is a fixed attribute, relatively impervious to manipulations by teachers, and that it does not take very long in school for teachers to disentangle a child's native ability from cultural factors related to race or socio-economic class. Moreover, middle and upper-class parents often strenuously resist de-tracking efforts for fear that their children will be educationally shortchanged by being grouped with inferior students, and that their educational futures are being put at risk for the sake of rigid egalitarian ends (Wells & Oakes, 1996). These fears are not entirely without empirical basis. Some studies on the effectiveness of homogeneous versus heterogeneous grouping practices for high-ability students have concluded that these students are slightly better served in homogeneous groups (Brewer et al., 1995; Hoffer, 1992; Kerckhoff, 1986). Even if this is true, however, proponents of de-tracking believe that this phenomenon would evaporate if teachers were trained to teach better. More specifically, Jeannie Oakes and Martin Lipton (1992) train teachers in heterogeneous classrooms to integrate disciplines rather than teaching subject by subject, to teach by projects rather than always out of a book, and to implement authentic assessment techniques rather than pencil and paper tests alone.

While the motivations of Oakes and her colleagues are admirable and their attention to improving teachers' instruction is valuable, I recommend the moderate approach to reforming ability-grouping practices in public schools. Educators should be very cautious about ability grouping in the elementary years because students have had little time to display their native abilities apart from social background influences. However, if students are only separated for short periods each day—in basic skills subjects where the range of student abilities is very high—and if students' placements are continuously re-assessed, it might be defensible. Robert Slavin (1991, 1987) seems to have it about right. Although Slavin is not opposed to highly fluid, within-class ability grouping for Reading, he criticizes more comprehensive separation practices and specializes in training teachers to use cooperative learning groups more effectively, where peer-teaching can occur and the teacher is not the sole possessor of the "answers." I do not include gifted and talented children in my recommendations, however. According to Chen-Lin Kulik and James A. Kulik (1987, 1982), they suffer in heterogeneous classrooms and deserve separate instruction throughout the day. I agree, so long as we are talking about a few children on the far right end of the bell curve and not using this term as a euphemism for a broad spectrum of socially advantaged children. Finally, I do not think that separate vocational and academic programs in high schools would be problematic if ability-grouping practices were more cautiously used before that time, and if instructional quality and ease of movement between programs were closely monitored.

Recommendation Three:
Reduce K-3 Class Size
and Elementary and Secondary School Size

We already place extraordinary demands on teachers in our society, and asking them to transcend their mainstream pedagogical styles while simultaneously moving toward heterogeneous instruction requires reciprocal efforts on the part of policymakers to make these changes manageable.[3] Unfortunately, the most commonsense solution to easing the burden on teachers, reducing class size, is among the most expensive. This disincentive is exacerbated by the fact that the research concerning the effects of reducing class size on student achievement has been ambiguous until recently. Like student-grouping practices, the achievement effects of alternative class sizes have been studied throughout the century. While early studies (for reviews of the early literature, see Blake, 1954; NEA, 1968) generally favored small class sizes, more recent studies have been more specific about when these effects are most significant, or indeed significant at all. A major meta-analysis of existing research on class size by G. Glass and M.L. Smith (1978) demonstrated that student numbers needed to dip below twenty before there was any appreciable difference in academic achievement, which would require a major infusion of funding for urban districts that often average over thirty students per teacher (Odden, 1990). In a descriptive review of the previous literature, Glen E. Robinson and J.H. Wittebols (1986) found a positive relationship between reduced class size and student achievement in the primary grades, but that this relationship became progressively weaker as students advance through school.

Those who believe that smaller class sizes cannot help but increase student performance over time have found hope in Tennessee's Project STAR (Student/Teacher Achievement Ratio; Word, et al., 1990, 1994), a recent study that Frederick Mosteller (et al., 1996) recently hailed as "one of the great experiments in education in U.S. history" (p. 814). Following the studies described above and financially supported by the Tennessee State Legislature, STAR investigators focused their study on grades K-3 and reduced the size of the experimental group classes significantly, from 23 students to 15. In each of 79 inner-city, urban, suburban, and rural schools across the state, K-3 teachers and students were randomly assigned to "large" or "small" classes, or "large" classes with an instructional aide. With more than 6,500 students and 330 teachers participating, the randomization technique assured that the treatment groups were relatively similar prior to the experiment, and the four-year duration of what they called Phase One (1985-1989) provided ample time for class-size differences to have their effects. The fact that the experiment involved different types of communities eliminated the possibility of confounding effects caused by demographic and cultural factors. At the end of grade three, the experimental group outperformed the control group by an average of 7 percentile points on the Stanford Achievement Test, which is a significant, if not a huge amount (Word, et al., 1990).

Moreover, Phase Two (1989-present) of Project STAR, called the Lasting Benefits Study, demonstrated that students who experienced small classes in grades K-3 retained their advantages in the fourth and fifth grades (Achilles, et al., 1993). In other words, the benefits of small K-3 classes did not quickly fade away after these students returned to regular size classes, which is often the case in educational experiments. Phase Three (1989-present) of the study, Project Challenge, is even more encouraging, especially in regard to our concern with non-mainstream students. Enthused about the positive findings of Phase One, but working with limited financial resources, the Tennessee State Legislature decided to direct its assistance to the seventeen poorest districts in the state, which not surprisingly experienced the highest drop-out rates. After four years of smaller K-3 class sizes, the grade two test scores in these seventeen states had moved up an average of 21 ranks in Reading and 29 ranks in Mathematics as compared with 138 other districts across the state. In 1993, the seventeen poorest districts in Tennessee performed above the state average in Mathematics achievement and slightly below the average in Reading achievement, both significant improvements over their 1990 rankings. This finding is consistent with Robinson and Wittebols' (1986) conclusion that poor and minority students benefit disproportionately from smaller class sizes. Since improving the academic achievement of non-mainstream students is a primary concern of this project, the importance of Tennessee's experiment with smaller class sizes should not be overlooked. Finally, President Clinton should be commended for forwarding to Congress the "Class-Size Reduction and Teacher Quality Act" in May of 1998, which proposed a federal initiative to reduce the average primary-level class size across the nation to 18 students. As of October of 1998, it appears that Congress will approve this important project, but it has not yet become law.

Lessons drawn from recent effective schools research and corresponding restructuring efforts have raised another size issue to prominence: elementary and secondary school size. Many researchers have questioned the traditional notion that large comprehensive high schools help students excel because more types of courses are offered and teachers can specialize in specific aspects of their fields (see Conant, 1967, for the traditional view). The majority of recent studies have contradicted the traditional assumption that there is a positive relationship between school size and student achievement, but these studies are divided on the question of whether or not the relationship is actually negative, or, as Valerie Lee put it: "smaller is better" (et al., 1997, p. 208; for diverse interpretations of the literature, see Howley, 1989; Plecki, 1991; Fowler, 1992). When one looks at the academic performance of disadvantaged students specifically, however, the evidence consistently supports smaller elementary and secondary schools (Summers & Wolfe, 1975; Friedkin & Necochea, 1988; McGiverin, Gillman, & Tillitski, 1989; Plecki, 1991; Huang & Howley, 1993; Howley, 1996; Lee & Smith, 1997). More specifically, the ideal size for schools serving large numbers of disadvantaged students seems to be around 200-250 for elementary schools and 600-900 for high schools. Many rural schools already operate within these constraints for obvious demographic reasons, but many urban schools are three or more times larger than is ideal (Miller, 1995). Deborah Meier (1995), founder of the Central Park East Secondary and Elementary Schools that serve 450 and 250 students respectively, has articulated the fairly straightforward reasons why small schools serve non-mainstream students better. She mentions a variety of advantages that small schools have over large schools when serving non-mainstream students, but the crux of her argument concerns issues of intimacy and accessibility:

> Every child is entitled to be in a school small enough that he or she can be known by name to every faculty member in the school and well known by at least a few of them, a school so small that family can easily come in and see the responsible adults, and the responsible adults can easily and quickly see each other. What size is that exactly? It can't be too small, but surely it can't be larger than a few hundred! If that strikes us as shocking, we might for a moment look at the size of the average elite independent private school and wonder why we haven't learned this lesson until now. (p. 40)

Recommendation Four: Expand and Improve Federal Compensatory Education Programs

Along with reduced class and school size, teachers working in high-poverty schools deserve additional instructional assistance.

Despite the fact that some strings always come with governmental funds, it is difficult to argue that federal assistance for high-poverty schools violates the constitutional authority of states. In fact, federal assistance targeted at disadvantaged students is perhaps the most valuable function of the Department of Education. Since the time of President Lyndon Johnson, Chapter One of the Elementary and Secondary Education Act (also called Title One at various times) and Head Start have been the core of federal efforts to better educate disadvantaged students (Stickney & Marcus, 1985). I believe that both of these programs, the popularity of which ebbs and flows in correspondence with Democratic power cycles in Washington, should be expanded. I will address Chapter One first. Chapter One is the largest compensatory education program funded by the federal government, accounting for more than one-fifth of the Department of Education's budget (Natriello, 1990). While there is some diversity of practice among schools that receive Chapter One funds, the most common intervention strategy is to pull-out under-achieving elementary school children from regular classrooms for small-group tutoring sessions run by specially trained teachers (Birman et al., 1987; Carter, 1984). The impact of traditional Chapter One programs on disadvantaged students' academic achievement has been disappointing. The Sustaining Effects Study (SES), the "largest and most comprehensive evaluation of the effectiveness of Title One ever undertaken" (Carter, 1984, p. 6), concluded that "Title One was effective for students who were only moderately disadvantaged but it did not improve the relative achievement of the most disadvantaged part of the school population" (quoted in Carter, p. 7). The conclusions of the SES study were consistent with other evaluations of the time (see Levine & Havighurst, 1984, for a synthesis) and have been confirmed by more recent research as well (Stringfield & Yoder, 1992; Puma, et al., 1993).

There have been some encouraging developments in the

Chapter One story, however. The Hawkins-Stafford Amendments of 1988 made Chapter One legislation concerning the use of funds more flexible than it had been before that time. Consistent with the general reform emphasis of recent times, some process regulations were softened in favor of an emphasis on outcomes. Taking immediate advantage of this increased flexibility, Slavin and his colleagues developed a model Chapter One program called Success for All (SFA) in 1988, which modifies the traditional approach in significant ways (Slavin, 1991). In essence, the SFA strategy focuses on preventing school failure by making the earliest experiences of non-mainstream students in kindergarten and primary school more productive, rather then remediating the problems of students who have already struggled and are often demoralized. SFA teachers pay special attention to Reading because reading skills are foundational to academic success. While all other subjects are taught in heterogeneous classrooms, Reading is taught in homogeneous but multi-age classrooms, which is an important difference between SFA and the traditional single-grade grouping practices that were criticized in Chapter Two. Within these roughly homogeneous groups, students engage in highly structured cooperative learning experiences that emphasize both individual and group accountability. Reading assessments are administered bi-monthly and struggling students receive short one-on-one tutoring sessions while their peers are studying social studies. These tutoring sessions are aligned with the regular Reading curriculum, which is meant to alleviate a major problem with traditional Chapter One programs: lack of coordination between classroom teachers and Chapter One tutors. Whether Chapter One teachers tutor small groups or teach in separate classrooms, they often deliver basic-skill instruction that does not complement the instruction that students receive during the remainder of the day (Madden et al., 1991; Ross et al., 1997). This amounts to de facto tracking, with all of the student morale problems that come with it.

A common criticism of SFA is that the focus on improving regular classroom instruction means that the most disadvantaged students are not the only students being served, whereas in traditional Chapter One programs they are isolated so that this is the case. I think that Slavin is correct when he replies that if the academic achievement of the most disadvantaged students can improve through modifying the instruction that they receive in regular classrooms, then criticizing SFA because other students happen to benefit from these improvements is perverse. And both internal and external evaluators have concluded that SFA is modestly improving the educational success rates of its target population in cities such as Baltimore, Memphis, and Fort Wayne, Indiana. Synthesizing SFA effect-level studies conducted between 1988 and 1994, Slavin concludes that the "average" fifth-grader who has been served throughout her elementary school career by SFA would occupy the 70th percentile for reading achievement in one of their control schools (et al., 1996). Also, an external evaluation of the Fort Wayne program shows that African-American students are disproportionately benefiting in relation to their Caucasian peers (Ross, Smith, & Casey, 1995). Even modestly positive results are encouraging because SFA is a Chapter One model, meaning that it can be operated within these funding constraints, which were about $500 per student each year during the late 1980s. As Miller (1995) points out, the results of a program like SFA would clearly be more dramatic if our society chose to invest greater resources into compensatory education.

Head Start is the pre-school complement to Chapter One services. As discussed in the second chapter, the founders of Head Start in 1965 had unrealistic hopes about changing children's academic futures by providing them with one summer-long pre-school experience (Zigler, 1983). Actually, Head Start children do make significant academic progress as a result of the program, but these newfound advantages over their nonparticipating peers do not last long, as the disappointing results of the well-known Westinghouse evaluation (Cicirelli, 1969) made clear and more recent evaluations have confirmed (Consortium for Longitudinal Studies, 1983; McKey, et al., 1985; Woodhead, 1988; Haskins, 1989). There are two lines of defense against the prominent "fading effects" criticism of Head Start. First, academic development is only one goal of the program, which simultaneously seeks to promote physical and mental health, social responsibility and competence, and better family environments for disadvantaged children (the fact that Head Start serves disadvantaged parents as well as their children is often overlooked). Regarding these non-academic goals, the research on Head Start's effectiveness is much more positive (see McKey, et al., 1985; Copple, Cline, & Smith, 1987), although this research has been over-shadowed by the famous long-term studies of the High/Scope Perry Pre-school Program, which have now followed its graduates to age twenty-seven, documented their disproportionately positive social and occupational outcomes, and actually calculated a cost-benefit ratio for society of 6 to 1 (see Schweinhart, Barnes, & Weikart, 1993). Second, even if we do focus on the cognitive outcomes of Head Start, it is silly to hold a pre-school program accountable for fade-out effects that occur while children are in elementary school. Head Start is a school readiness program, and if children's academic skills are enhanced as a result of enrollment, then it is serving its function regardless of the elementary school system's inability to sustain these gains (see Zigler, 1994). Surely, Head Start can be improved, particularly in the area of teacher training and remuneration. It is difficult to attract and retain high quality teachers when the average annual salary is $15,000 per year. It is a valuable program, however, and it needs to reach more than the 30% of eligible children it served as of the early 1990s (Committee For Economic Development, 1991).

If Head Start were to receive full funding, as President

Clinton gestured toward early in his tenure, it would represent a significant step in the direction of substantive equality of educational opportunity. While I am not confident that our society will muster the moral and political will to address inequality of opportunity in such a substantial way, the cause must continually be argued, and Head Start is an important rallying point for two reasons. First, Head Start is about children. As I have argued throughout this book and will underline below, long-term social reform strategies should focus on those who have their lives ahead of them so that undesirable social outcomes can be prevented rather than merely alleviated after they occur. Second, Head Start's focus on the whole child—her physical and mental health, her social and emotional well-being, and her parents' capacity to provide for her—makes good sense. It might be argued that this is the role of family alone and does not require public support, but this is to ignore the crushing realities of joblessness, isolation, and violence that inner-city families face. Indeed, Ruby Takanishi and Patrick H. DeLeon (1994), upon reflecting on Head Start's future in the next quarter-century, point out that economic and social conditions have worsened markedly in the inner-cities since Head Start began, making public assistance even more necessary than before. Given this reality, Head Start services should be as comprehensive as possible, not simply aimed at raising the I.Q.'s of poor and minority children, but preparing them physically, mentally, and emotionally to enter elementary schools. Project Follow Through was established in 1967 to aid Head Start children in this transition, continuing support services until they reached the third grade. Project Follow Through never became a stable program, but the idea of transition services arose again with Senator Edward Kennedy's (1993) introduction of the Head Start Transition Project, which has recently been piloted in 32 demonstration sites (see Doernberger & Zigler, 1993). I recommend that we give these efforts our full support.

Recommendation Five:
Incorporate School Reform
into Broader Social Reform

This brings me to my final recommendation, which is less directly related to teaching and learning than the previous four, but is a critical pre-condition of equal educational opportunity: education reform must be complemented by broader social and economic reform. The most well-known articulation of this reminder is Henry J. Perkinson's book, *The Imperfect Panacea: American Faith in Education 1865-1965* (1968). As the title of Perkinson's book implies, Americans have always placed too much faith in the capacity of public schooling to equalize opportunities in the absence of other social policies that meet the basic human needs of poor children, such as good health care, nutrition, shelter, and clothing. We cannot expect the 21 percent of America's children who live in poverty—much less the 100,000 children who are without homes—to perform very well in school without meeting their basic needs (Kassebaum, 1994). This combination of unrealistic expectations and neglect of the pre-conditions of equal educational opportunity has produced in Americans a schizophrenic attitude regarding their schools: we grossly over-estimate their potential (in the current context) and then blame them for failing us. This irony has even played out in my book. I have just finished praising the potential of Chapter One and Head Start, the primary pieces of President Lyndon Johnson's educational strategy during the Great Society campaign, and arguably the key pieces of the campaign as a whole. I have recommended that we recover the commitment to substantive equality of educational opportunity that characterized the 1960s and 1970s. However, as articulated briefly in Chapter Four, Johnson's very advocacy of education reform was a political strategy that allowed him to avoid considering a more expensive commitment to broader income-redistribution programs (Kantor & Lowe, 1995). While Johnson's educational policies were admirable in comparison with his predecessors and successors, they fell far short of the requirements of authentic equality of opportunity as outlined in this project.

In *An American Imperative: Accelerating Minority Educational Advancement* (1995), Miller presents a comprehensive strategy for improving educational and occupational opportunities for disadvantaged children. Besides offering a number of education-specific strategies for realizing authentic equality of opportunity in American society, Miller advances a broader strategy of "social policy mobilization" that addresses areas such as job creation, health care, and the provision of an adequate safety net in terms of food, clothing, and housing (p. 342). A complete discussion of Miller's proposed social policies is beyond my purposes here, but I do wish to connect the task of general social reform to my ongoing concern with opportunity-to-learn standards. As Kevin Dougherty (1996) rightly observes, the definitions of OTL standards included in reform documents such as *Goals 2000*, even before Republicans engineered their removal, did not sufficiently attend to those "extra-school" inequalities that affect students' readiness to profit from schooling (p. 48). It would be wonderful if some individual state chose to take the lead in authentic education reform by constructing a specific (but not necessarily lengthy or overly intrusive) set of OTL standards that takes broader social stratification issues into account, and aligns educational strategies with other human capital-oriented services such as those that provide medical, social, and legal services for children who need them. As argued throughout this project, an authentically meritocratic educational system must address both inequities within the school system and those deeper socio-structural and economic inequalities that skew the educational "race" from the outset.

Can Schooling
Make a Difference?

Recall from Chapter Four that the consistent findings of the "schools don't make a difference" research of the 1960s and early 1970s demonstrated that American public schooling, as traditionally practiced, did little to narrow the cognitive achievement gap between disadvantaged children and their more advantaged peers. Moreover, increasing the levels of large-scale inputs—such as improved facilities, instructional materials, and teacher salaries—does not alleviate the problem apart from significant changes in the conduct of teaching and learning. I have not attempted to re-assess these empirical questions here. Rather, following the logic—if not always the actual recommendations—of the effective schools movement, I have tried to identify specific practices that have shown empirical promise for poor and ethnic-minority students. I believe that the recommendations advanced above can make a positive difference in these students' academic achievement, and their subsequent academic attainment and occupational performance as well. I also wish to point out that just because the recommendations above were justified solely in terms of achievement effects does not mean that they are not justifiable on other grounds, such as self-esteem, enjoyment of schooling, and future aspirations. There is substantial empirical literature that addresses non-cognitive outcomes, which are obviously important even if they are slightly less central to the conduct of schooling than are learning outcomes.

Finally, in concluding this recommendations section, I want to relate some remarks that Daniel Levine (1990) made upon completing a substantial review of the school effectiveness literature. After citing a list of conditions and practices that characterized schools which produced unusual levels of student-achievement, Levine turned to the affective attributes of successful reformers.

To summarize briefly, Levine encouraged educators to be insistent on positive learning outcomes for all students, persistent in doing what must be done to obtain these outcomes, resilient in moving forward when problems emerge, and consistent in providing coordinated and coherent instructional programs. Levine's focus has been on raising academic achievement for all students as opposed to concentrating on disadvantaged students specifically, but I think his more general advice is fitting. I turn now to some final philosophical exhortations.

III. The Intuitive Appeal of Equality of Opportunity as a Distributive Principle

Our Intuitions Regarding the Equal Moral Worth of Persons

Before concluding the project, I want to fortify the foregoing arguments for the moral and philosophical supremacy of substantive equality of opportunity, or authentic meritocracy, by appealing to our most basic, almost visceral inclinations regarding human nature and the proper organization of societies. Recall from the opening chapter Charles Taylor's claim that moral and political philosophy is most productive when it begins with what he calls our "commonsense understandings" (quoted earlier, p. 20; 1983, p. 62). One of the most crucial claims of the historic liberal tradition that coheres with most Americans' common-sense notions concerns the equal moral worth of persons. As discussed in Chapter Three, all human beings share a capacity for rationality that sets them apart from other creatures. Related to this capacity for rationality, all human beings—at least those who are not pathologically ill—experience certain powerful but predictable sentiments, such as love and grief, an aversion to pain, and an attraction to pleasure. Given that these attributes are universal across the human species, and largely unique to it, one can conclude that human beings are more alike one another than they are different, and that they share an imperfect but essential equality.

Earlier in the liberal story, this intuitive understanding of human equality was thought to be adequately respected by the simple principle of negative liberty, or formal equality of opportunity that ensured the absence of economic discrimination on the basis of morally irrelevant background characteristics such as racial or ethnic identity. In the last century, however, what Amy Gutmann describes as "a relatively new liberal awareness of the material prerequisites for equalizing opportunity among individuals" has caused the displacement of the negative conception of liberty by a positive conception, and the formal interpretation of equality of opportunity has given way to the substantive conception as advanced in this book (1980, p, 218). While the move to positive liberty and authentic meritocracy might demand sacrifices on the part of privileged citizens that run counter to their self-interests, I think it becomes evident upon reflection that respecting human equality requires that we do what we can to ensure that each person born into American society possesses life chances that are comparable to her peers.

Our Intuitions Regarding Individual Agency and Responsibility

Another crucial claim of the historic liberal tradition that coheres with most Americans' deepest convictions concerns the relationship between individual liberty and personal responsibility. According to traditional liberals and the vast majority of lay citizens, every individual deserves a reasonable chance for educational and economic success, but no individuals deserve more than minimal handouts, at least for their own personal consumption. Even though the substantive interpretation of equality of opportunity advanced here calls for significant redistribution of wealth on behalf of poor families, the nature of the recommended investments are always human capital-related and designed to help children compete economically upon reaching adulthood. This is not to recant my previous acceptance of Rawls' argument that hard-working but under-talented adults deserve some social rewards, but it does exclude those who make little effort. As Dworkin states, the ideal distributive system is "ambition sensitive" and "endowment insensitive" (quoted earlier, p. 96; 1981, p. 311). But these two characteristics are often impossible to separate in practice. I think that Strike's solution— limiting the variance in social rewards apportioned to "successful" and "unsuccessful" persons so that these rewards do not distort competition for their children—is the best way to approach the problem. The main point, however, is that substantive equality of opportunity successfully negotiates the tension between social equality and individual responsibility. We want to treat people equally, but we do not want to give anyone a free ride.

Our Intuitions Regarding Making Investments in Children

Finally, I wish to make one last appeal to our moral intuitions regarding the human experience and the fairest arrangement of society, and to shift the focus to educational concerns specifically. I argued in the third chapter that the substantive interpretation of equality of opportunity is not directly manipulative, but is rather interventionist in nature, meaning that equality of occupational results across racial or ethnic groups is not to be directly brought about through affirmative action programs of some type, but is simply a long-term goal to be approached through significant and continuous human capital-related investments in young persons. I believe that ear-marking the bulk of our social expenditures toward the development of the youth of our society—whose lives are affected so profoundly by the physical, emotional, and intellectual nurturance they do or do not receive in their earliest years—makes good sense. An example from American educational history illustrates this point. Horace Mann, the Secretary of the Massachusetts Board of Education between 1837 and 1848 and the leading public school educator of the nineteenth century, made some interesting remarks when he surprised his peers by leaving a promising legislative career for a new and comparatively unprestigious position in the state's new Education Department. Always a zealous humanitarian reformer—focusing until that time on overturning the state's debtor laws, the temperance movement, and the treatment of the mentally ill—Mann had grown disillusioned with the possibility of altering the attitudes and habits of adults, but his pessimism did not extend to the young: "Having found the present generation composed of materials almost unmalleable, I am transferring my efforts to the next. Men are cast iron; but children are wax. Strength expended upon the latter may be effectual, which will make no impression on the former" (quoted in Tozer et al., 1998, p. 57). Mann's perceptions are as accurate today as they were in his time. Egalitarian social change is only possible if we focus on the next generation and prevent future disillusionment and moral resignation by creating hopeful futures for children born into disadvantaged situations. As the unquestioned centerpiece of human capital-related developmental institutions in our society, authentically meritocratic educational systems are of paramount importance.

IV. Conclusion:
Equal Educational Opportunity
and Excellence in the Good Society

In closing, I wish to revisit a question that was asked in the opening chapter: How might educational excellence and equality of opportunity be reconciled in a more legitimate manner than it has been in the recent past? Recall from the opening chapter that Thomas E. Schaefer criticized the major reform documents of the excellence movement for falsely proclaiming an "easy complementarity" between the two ideals, naively, or perhaps disingenuously, assuming that simply raising the academic achievement bar—in the form of newly articulated curriculum standards with high stakes assessments attached to them—would provide sufficient direction and motivation for schools and students to realize in practice the slogan of "excellence for all" (1990, p. 41). Recall also that Republican and Southern Democratic resistance to President Clinton's signature education bill in 1994 dictated that states would not be required to submit opportunity-to-learn standards alongside their curriculum and assessment plans when applying for *Goals 2000* funding, and that the OTL language disappeared completely upon the bill's second reauthorization. Moreover, as Kevin J. Dougherty (1996) notes, the discussion of OTL standards at the federal level never addressed systemic school policies such as curricular tracking that disproportionately relegate poor and minority students to the bottom levels, nor did it engage the discussion about what educational systems must do to counter-balance educational inequalities arising from non-school sources such as parents' education levels and neighborhood culture.

It is true, as both Schaefer and Gutmann (1980) point out, that the concept of equality—and, by extension, equality of opportunity—is metaphysically parasitic, and depends upon some companion concept like liberty or excellence for its utility. However, if one thinks in a temporal rather than a metaphysical sense, the relationship of priority is reversed. Ultimately, what particular persons in particular cultures choose to call excellent is always defined in relative terms, and actually connotes some comparative meaning like "better than we usually see it," or "better than the rest." Thus, if we know that a certain portion of the youth population is systematically disadvantaged in school by virtue of poverty or non-mainstream status, it is difficult to conclude that their more privileged peers are out-performing them purely as a result of their excellent abilities or efforts. It is also difficult to label as excellent any educational institution in which certain types of students disproportionately succeed and other types disproportionately fail. In short, equality of educational opportunity—equal chances of academic success for all— must exist before we can conclusively identify either individual or institutional excellence.

Actually, the educational aims of a perfectly just society—a hypothetical but conceptually useful tool that philosophers like to call the "good society"—would share many similarities with the major reform documents of the last two decades, particularly those of the 1990s. For instance, identifying specific curricular standards for students across the K-12 spectrum—including both content-specific and cognitive-processing targets that both teachers and their students can work toward—is fundamental to educational excellence and represents a significant pedagogical advancement over previous years. Also like the reform documents of the last two decades, the educational aims of the good society would proudly proclaim excellence for all. However, the essential difference between the educational aims of the good society and those of our own might simply be that the former's vision of excellence for all is articulated in good faith, whereas the latter's claim to the same is merely empty rhetoric.

In terms of formal educational opportunities in the good

society, disparities in facilities, instructional materials, and teacher-quality between wealthy and poor communities would not exist, as the Supreme Courts in fifteen actual American states have declared must become the case (see Hickrod, 1997). As for the more substantive interpretation of equal educational opportunity advanced here, however, any parallels between the hypothetical good society and actual practices in America are much harder to come by, although New Jersey has taken some positive steps. The crippling hold that entrenched socio-structural and economic inequalities possess over the educational "meritocracy" in this country has scarcely been challenged. As described in the opening chapter, President Clinton wishes to harvest the human capital present in our nation's schools for the purpose of improving our international economic competitiveness (Smith & Scoll, 1995). However, he is not willing to acknowledge the radical alterations of the social and economic order that would be required if his guiding motives for increasing human capital were justice-oriented rather than utilitarian, attentive to individual outcomes rather than mean test scores, and authentically liberal rather than politically expedient. Clinton would do well to reflect upon Immanuel Kant's (1948) injunction that individual persons—especially children—are always to be treated as inviolable ends, and never as means to someone else's ends.

Finally, some might argue that the dramatic disparity between the social and educational vision advanced in this work and the political realities just described should compel me to pick a more modest battle. I would disagree. The guiding purpose of this work has been to re-visit one aspect of the good society - the existence of an authentically meritocratic educational system— and to consider how it might be realized in practice if in some future day we summon the moral and political will to do so. If the sole effect of this book is to pique one reader's conscience, or even just my own, the effort has not been in vain. The same can be said about moral philosophy in general. It is always important to nurture our souls.

Notes

1. Recall from Chapter Two that the interactionist perpective does not blame schools alone for the struggles of non-mainstream students and acknowledges that many of these students arrive at school unprepared to learn.
2. I must acknowledge that Tharp's experiments with culturally responsive instruction have taken place in contexts in which the receiving audiences, while not of mainstream identity, are homogeneous. Clearly, teachers in a culturally heterogeneous environment cannot tailor their instruction to any single ethnic group, but must balance the needs of different ethnic groups. However, Tharp has identified two principles for teaching non-mainstream children in general: immerse them in oral and written language as extensively and creatively as possible, and contextualize instruction so that it relates to their personal experiences. Obviously, the latter requirement is not possible for all children at all times, but any move away from a mainstream ethno-centric approach is positive (1994).
3. As stated in Chapter Two, I am referring to the majority of the teaching force. A solid minority of teachers come from non-mainstream backgrounds.

References

Aaron, Henry. *Politics and the Professors: The Great Society in Perspective*. Washington, DC: The Brookings Institution, 1978.

Achilles, C.M., Nye, B.A., Zaharias, J.B., & Fulton, B.D. *The Lasting Benefits Study (LBS) in Grades 4 and 5 (1990-1991): A Legacy From Tennessee's Four-Year (K-3) Class-Size Study (1985-1989), Project STAR*. Paper presented at a meeting of the North Carolina Association for Research in Education (NCARE), Greensboro, NC, 1993.

Alexander, K.L., Eckland, Bruce K., & Griffin, Larry J. The Wisconsin Model of Socio-Economic Achievement: A Replication. *American Journal of Sociology*, Vol. 81, 1975.

Alexander, K.L., Cook, M.A., & McDill, E.L. Curriculum Tracking and Educational Stratification. *American Sociological Review*, Vol. 43, 1978.

Alexander, K.L., & Cook, M.A. Curricula and Coursework: A Surprise Ending to a Familiar Story. *American Sociological Review*, Vol. 47, 1982.

Alexander, K.L., & McDill, E.L. Selection and Allocation Within Schools: Some Causes and Consequences of Curriculum Placement. *American Sociological Review*, Vol. 41, 1976.

American Association of Colleges for Teacher Education. *Recruiting Minority Teachers: A Practical Guide*. Washington, DC: American Association of Colleges for Teacher Education, 1989.

American Federation of Teachers. *Making Standards Matter.* Washington, DC: American Federation of Teachers, 1997.

Appiah, Robert Anthony. *In My Father's House: Africa in the Philosophy of Culture.* London, UK: Oxford University Press, 1992.

Apple, Michael. Producing Inequality: Ideology and Economy in the National Reports on Education. *Educational Studies,* 1986.

Apple, Michael. Educational Reform and Educational Crisis. *Journal of Research in Science Teaching,* Vol. 29, No. 8, 1992.

Applebee, A.N., Langer, J.A., & Mullis, I.V.S. *Who Reads Best? Factors Related to Reading Achievement in Grades 3, 7, and 11.* Princeton, NJ: Educational Testing Service, 1988.

Aristotle. *The Politics.* Ernest Barker, ed. London, UK: Oxford University Press, 1946.

Arons, Stephen. The Threat to Freedom in Goals 2000. In N. Cobb, ed., *The Future of Education.* New York: The College Board, 1994.

Averch, Harvey A. et al. *How Effective is Schooling?* Santa Monica, CA: Rand Corporation, 1972.

Baratz, S.S., & Baratz, J.C. Early Childhood Intervention: The Social Science Base of Institutional Racism. *Harvard Educational Review,* Vol. 40, 1970.

Barber, Benjamin R., & Battistoni, Richard M. *Education For Democracy: A Sourcebook for Students and Teachers.* Duboque, IA: Kendall/ Hunt Publishing, 1993.

Barro S., & Kolstad, A. *Who Drops Out of High School? Findings from High School and Beyond* (Report No. CS 87-397c). Washington, DC: U.S. Department of Education, National Center For Education Statistics, 1987.

Barton, Paul E., Coley, Richard J., & Goertz, Margaret E. *The State of Inequality.* Princeton, NJ: Educational Testing Service, 1991.

Belke, T.W. A Synopsis of Herrnstein and Murray's *The Bell Curve: Intelligence and Class Structure in American Life. The Alberta Journal of Educational Research,* Vol. XLI, No. 3, 1995.

Bell, Daniel. On Meritocracy and Equality. *Public Interest,* Fall, 1972.

Bennett, K.P., & LeCompte M.D. *The Way Schools Work.* New York: Longman Press, 1990.

Bentham, Jeremy. *Introduction to Principles of Morals and Legislation. Works,* vol. 1. John Bowring, ed. Edinburgh, UK: 1843.

Bereiter, Carl. The Changing Face of Educational Disadvantagement.

Phi Delta Kappan, April, 1985.

Berlin, Isaiah. Two Concepts of Liberty. From *Four Essays on Liberty.* Oxford, UK: Oxford University Press, 1969.

Berliner, David, & Biddle, Bruce J. *The Manufactured Crisis.* New York: Addison-Wesley Publishing, 1995.

Bianchi, S.M. Children's Progress Through School: A Research Note. *Sociology of Education,* Vol. 57, 1984.

Birman, B., Orland, M., Jung, R., Anson, R., Garcia, G., Moore, M., Funkhouser, J., Morrison, D., Turnbull, B., & Reisner, E. *The Current Operation of the Chapter 1 Program.* Washington, DC: U.S. Department of Education, Office of Educational Research and Improvement, 1987.

Blake, Howard V. Class Size: A Summary of Selected Studies in Elementary and Secondary Schools. Ed.D. Dissertation. Teachers College, Columbia University, 1954.

Blaug, M. The Correlation Between Education and Earnings: What Does It Signify? *Higher Education,* Vol. 1, No. 1, 1972.

Bourdieu, Pierre, & Passeron, Jean-Claude. Reproduction in Education, Society, and Culture. *SAGE Studies in Social and Educational Change,* Vol. 5, 1977.

Bowles, Samuel, & Gintis, Herbert. *Schooling in Capitalist America.* New York: Basic Books, 1976.

Boyer, Ernest L. *High School: A Report on Secondary Education in America.* New York: Harper & Row, 1983.

Boykin, A. Wade. Task Variability and the Performance of Black and White Children: Vervistic Explorations. *Journal of Black Studies,* Vol. 12, 1982.

Bracey, Gerald W. Why Can't They Be Like We Were? *Phi Delta Kappan,* October, 1991.

Braddock, Jomills Henry, II, & McPartland, James. Alternatives to Tracking on the Agenda for Restructuring Schools. *Educational Leadership,* Vol. 47, 1990.

Brewer, Dominic J., Rees, Daniel I., & Argys, Laura M. Detracking America's Schools: The Reform Without Cost? *Phi Delta Kappan,* Vol. 77, 1995.

Brice-Heath, Shirley. Questioning at Home and at School: A Comparative Study. In G. Spindler, ed. *Doing the Ethnography of Schooling.* New York: Holt, Rinehart, & Winston, 1982.

Brooks, Charlotte. Some Approaches to Teaching English as a Second Language. In S.W. Webster, ed., *The Disadvantaged Learner*. San Francisco, CA: Chandler, 1966.

Brown v. Board of Education of Topeka, Kansas, 347 U.S. 483. 1954.

Bruno, R.R. *School Enrollment—Social and Economic Characteristics of Students: October 1986* (U.S. Bureau of the Census, Current Population Reports, Series P-20, No. 429). Washington, DC: U.S. Government Printing Office, 1988.

Burbules, Nicholas, Lord, Brian T., & Sherman, Ann L. Equity, Equal Opportunity, and Education. *Educational Evaluation and Policy Analysis*, Vol. 4, No. 2, 1982.

Burbules, Nicholas, & Sherman, Ann L. Equal Educational Opportunity: Ideal or Ideology. *Proceedings of the Philosophy of Education Society*, 1979.

Calfee, R.C., Cazden, C.B., Duran, R.P., Griffin, M.P., Martus, M., & Willis, H.D. *Designing Reading Instruction For Cultural Minorities: The Case of the Kamehameha Education Program*. Cambridge, MA: The Harvard Graduate School of Education, 1981.

Campbell, Duane E. *Choosing Democracy: A Practical Guide to Multicultural Education*. Englewood Cliffs, NJ: Merrill Publishing, 1996.

Carter, L.F. The Sustaining Effects of Compensatory and Elementary Education. *Educational Researcher*, Vol. 13, 1984.

Cicirelli, V.G. *The Impact of Head Start: An Evaluation of the Effects of Head Start on Children's Cognitive and Affective Development*. (Report presented to the Office of Economic Opportunity, No. PB 184-328). Washington, DC: Westinghouse Learning Corporation, 1969.

Cicourel, A.V., & Kitsuse, J. *The Educational Decision Makers*. Indianapolis, IN: Bobbs-Merrill, 1963.

Clark, Burton R. The "Cooling Out" Function in Higher Education. *American Journal of Sociology*, Vol. 65, No. 6, 1960.

Clark, Burton R. *Educating the Expert Society*. San Francisco, CA: Chandler, 1961.

Clark, K.B. The Cult of Cultural Deprivation: A Complex Social Psychological Phenomenon. In K.B. Clark, ed., *Environmental Deprivation and Enrichment*. New York: Ferkhauf Graduate School of Education, Yeshiva University, 1965.

Clark, K.B. Cultural Deprivation Theories: The Social and Psychological Limitations. In K.B. Clark, M. Deutsch, A. Gartner, F. Keppel,

H. Lewis, T. Pettigrew, L. Plotkin, & F. Riessman. *The Education-ally Deprived: The Potential for Change*. New York: Metropolitan Applied Research Center, 1972.

Clune, William H. The Best Path to Systemic Educational Policy: Standard/Centralized or Differentiated/Decentralized? *Educational Evaluation and Policy Analysis*, Vol. 15, 1993.

Clune, William H. The Shift from Equity to Adequacy in School Finance. *Educational Policy*, Vol. 8, No. 4, 1994.

Cohen, Marshall. Berlin and the Liberal Tradition. *Philosophical Quarterly*, Vol. 10, 1960.

Coleman, James, et al. *Equality of Educational Opportunity*. Washington, DC: U.S. Government Printing Office, 1966.

Coleman, James. The Concept of Equality of Educational Opportunity. *Equal Educational Opportunity: Harvard Educational Review*, 1968.

Coleman, James. Equality of Opportunity and Equality of Results. *Harvard Educational Review*, Vol. 43, No. 1, 1973.

Coleman, James. Equal Educational Opportunity: A Definition. *Oxford Review of Education*, Vol. 1, No. 1, 1975.

Collins, Randall. Functional and Conflict Theories of Educational Stratification. *American Sociological Review*, Vol. 36, 1971.

Collins, Randall. *The Credential Society: An Historical Sociology of Education*. New York: Academic Press, Inc., 1979.

Committee For Economic Development. *The Unfinished Agenda: A New Vision For Child Development and Education*. New York: Committee For Economic Development, 1991.

Commonwealth of Kentucky. *State Improvement Plan: Goals 2000: Educate America Act* —Year II Funding. Frankfort, KY: Commonwealth of Kentucky, 1995.

Conant, James Bryant. *Slums and Suburbs: A Commentary on Schools in Metropolitan Areas*. New York: McGraw-Hill, 1961.

Conant, James Bryant. *The Comprehensive High School*. New York: McGraw-Hill, 1967.

Consortium for Longitudinal Studies. *As the Twig is Bent: Lasting Effects of Pre-School Programs*. Hillsdale, NJ: Erlbaum, 1983.

Cookson, Jr., Peter. Goals 2000: Framework for the New Educational Federalism. *Teachers College Record*, Vol. 96, No. 3, 1995.

Copple, C., Cline, M., & Smith, A. *Paths to the Future: Long-Term Effects of Head Start in the Philadelphia School District*. Washington, DC: U.S. Department of Health and Human Services, 1987.

Council of Chief State School Officers. *Status Report: State Systemic Education Improvements.* Washington DC: Council of Chief State School Officers, 1995.

Council of Chief State School Officers. *Mathematics and Science Content Standards and Curriculum Frameworks: States' Progress on Development and Implementation.* Washington, DC: Council of Chief State School Officers, 1997.

Cremin, Lawrence A. *Popular Education and Its Discontents.* New York: Harper and Row, 1990.

Dalton, Stephanie, Tharp, Roland, & Blaine, Daniel. *Pre-Service Education For Teachers of Minorities: The Hawaii University / Schools Partnership Program.* Washington, DC: American Educational Research Association, 1987.

Darling-Hammond, Linda. National Standards and Assessments: Will They Improve Anything? *American Journal of Education,* Vol. 102, 1994.

Delpit, Lisa. The Silenced Dialogue: Power and Pedagogy in Educating Other People's Children. *Harvard Educational Review,* August, 1988.

Diegmueller, Karen, & Lawton, Millicent. Conferees Seek to Overcome Barriers to Standards Reform. *Education Week,* May 29, 1996.

Doerngerger, C., & Zigler, E. Project Follow Through: Intent and Reality. In E. Zigler & S. J. Styfco, eds. *Head Start and Beyond: A National Plan for Extended Childhood Intervention.* New Haven, CT: Yale University Press, 1993.

Dougherty, Kevin J. Opportunity-to-Learn Standards: A Sociological Critique. *Sociology of Education,* Extra issue, 1996.

Dworkin, Ronald. What is Equality? Equality of Resources. *Philosophy and Public Affairs,* Vol. 10, No. 4, 1981.

Eder, Donna. Ability Grouping as a Self-Fulfilling Prophecy: A Micro-Analysis of Teacher-Student Interaction. *Sociology of Education,* Vol. 54, 1981.

Ellwood, D.T. *Poor Support: Poverty in the American Family.* New York: Basic Books, 1988.

Elmore, Richard F., & Fuhrman, Susan H. Opportunity-to-Learn Standards and the State Role in Education. *Teachers College Record,* Vol. 96, No. 3, 1995.

Ennis, Robert. Equality of Educational Opportunity. *Educational Theory,*

Vol. 26, No. 1, 1976.

Erickson, Frederick. Transformation and School Success: The Politics and Culture of Educational Achievement. *Anthropology and Education Quarterly,* December, 1987.

Farrell Jr., Walter C., Johnson Jr., James H., Sapp, Marty, & Jones, Cloyzelle K. *The Bell Curve:* Ringing in the Contract with America. *Educational Leadership,* April, 1995.

Feuerstein, Reuven, & Kozulin, Alex. *The Bell Curve:* Getting the Facts Straight. *Educational Leadership,* April, 1995.

Finn Jr., Chester E. The Future of Education's Liberal Consensus. *Change,* September, 1980.

Fishkin, James. *Justice, Equal Opportunity, and the Family.* New Haven, CT: Yale University Press, 1983.

Fowler, William J., Jr. What Do We Know About School Size? What Should We Know? A paper presented at the annual meeting of the American Educational Research Association, April 20-24, 1992.

Frankel, Charles. Equality of Opportunity. *Ethics,* Vol. 81, No. 3, 1971.

Fraser, Steven, ed. *The Bell Curve Wars: Race, Intelligence, and the Future of America.* New York: Basic Books, 1995.

Freire, Paulo. *Pedagogy of the Oppressed.* New York: The Seabury Press, 1970.

Friedkin, N., & Necochea, J. School System Design and Performance: A Contingency Perspective. *Educational Evaluation and Policy Analysis,* Vol. 10, 1988.

Friedman, N.L. Cultural Deprivation: A Commentary in the Sociology of Knowledge. In J.L. Frost & G.R. Hawkes, eds. *The Disadvantaged Child: Issues and Innovations.* Boston, MA: Houghton Mifflin, 1970.

Galston, William. Equality of Opportunity and Liberal Theory. In Frank S. Lucash, ed. *Justice and Equality Here and Now.* Ithaca, NY: Cornell University Press, 1986.

Gamoran, Adam. Instructional and Institutional Effects of Ability Groupings. *Sociology of Education,* Vol. 59, 1986.

Gamoran, Adam. The Variable Effects of High School Tracking. *American Sociological Review,* Vol. 57, 1992.

Gamoran, Adam. The Stratification of High School Learning Opportunities. *Sociology of Education,* Vol. 60, 1987.

Gamoran, Adam, & Berends, Mark. The Effects of Stratification in Secondary Schools: Synthesis of Survey and Ethnographic Research. *Review of Educational Research*, Vol. 57, No. 4, 1987.

Gamoran, Adam. Rank, Performance, and Mobility in Elementary School Grouping. *Sociological Quarterly*, Vol. 30, No. 1, 1989.

Gamoran, Adam, & Mare, Robert D. Secondary School Tracking and Educational Inequality: Compensation, Reinforcement, or Neutrality. *American Journal of Sociology*, Vol. 94, No. 5, 1989.

Gardner, Howard. *Frames of Mind*. New York: Basic Books, 1987.

Gardner, Howard. *Multiple Intelligences: The Theory Into Practice*. New York: Basic Books, 1993.

Gay, Geneva. Educational Equality For Students of Color. In James A. Banks & Cherry A. McGee Banks, eds. *Multicultural Education: Issues and Perspectives*. Boston, MA: Allyn & Bacon, 1997.

Gay, Geneva. The Relationship Between Multicultural and Democratic Education. *Social Studies*, Vol. 88, No. 1, 1997.

Gerth, Hans, & C. Wright Mills, eds. *From Max Weber: Essays in Sociology*. London, UK: Routledge, Kegan, & Paul, 1948.

Glass, G., & Smith, M.L. *Meta-Analysis of the Relationship of Class Size and Student Achievement*. San Francisco, CA: Far West Laboratory for Educational Research, 1978.

Glendon, Mary Ann. *Rights Talk: The Impoverishment of Political Discourse*. New York: The Free Press, 1991.

Glenn, B.C. Excellence and Equity: Implications for Effective Schools. *Journal of Negro Education*, Vol. 54.

Goodlad, John I. *A Place Called School: Prospects for the Future*. New York: McGraw-Hill, 1984.

Gould, Stephen Jay. *The Mismeasure of Man*. New York: Norton, 1981.

Gould, Stephen Jay. Curveball. *New Yorker*, November, 15, 1994.

Grant, Linda. Black Females' "Place" in Desegregated Classrooms. *Sociology of Education,* April, 1984.

Green, Thomas F. Equal Educational Opportunity: The Durable Injustice. In Charles A. Tesconi & E. Hurwitz, eds. *Education for Whom?* New York: Dodd, Mead, 1974.

Green, Thomas H. Liberal Legislation and Freedom of Contract. (1888). In R.L. Nettleship, ed. *Works of Thomas Hill Green, Vol. III*. Abridged by D. Miller in *Liberty*. Oxford, UK: Oxford University Press, 1991.

Gross, Barry. Real Equality of Opportunity. In Ellen Frankel Paul et al., ed. *Equal Opportunity*. New York: Basil Blackwell, 1987.

Guiton, Gretchen, & Oakes, Jeannie. Opportunity to Learn and Conceptions of Educational Equality. *Educational Evaluation and Policy Analysis*, Vol. 17, No. 3, 1995.

Gutmann, Amy. *Liberal Equality*. Cambridge, UK: Cambridge University Press, 1980.

Gutmann, Amy. Communitarian Critics of Liberalism. *Philosophy and Public Affairs*, Summer, 1985.

Gutmann, Amy. *Democratic Education*. Princeton, NJ: Princeton University Press, 1987.

Gutmann, Amy. Distributing Public Education in a Democracy. In Amy Gutmann, ed. *Democracy and the Welfare State*. Princeton, NJ: Princeton University Press, 1988.

Haller, E.J., & Davis, S.A. Does Socioeconomic Status Bias the Assignment of Elementary School Students to Reading Groups? *American Educational Research Journal*, Vol. 17, No. 4, 1980.

Haller, E.J., & Davis, S.A. Teacher Perceptions, Parental Social Status, and Grouping for Reading Instruction. *Sociology of Education*, Vol. 54, 1981.

Haller, E.J. Pupil Race and Elementary School Ability Grouping: Are Teachers Biased Against Black Children? *American Educational Research Journal*, Vol. 22, No. 4, 1985.

Hallinan, Maureen, & Sorensen, Aage B. Ability Grouping and Student Friendships. *American Educational Research Journal*, Vol. 22, 1985.

Hallinan, Maureen, & Sorensen, Aage B. Tracking: From Theory to Practice. *Sociology of Education*, Vol. 67, 1994.

Hanushek, Eric A. Moving Beyond School Spending Fetishes. *Educational Leadership*, Vol. 53, No. 3, 1995.

Harp, Lonnie. Equity Debates in States Shift To Standards and Technology. *Education Week*, March, 6, 1996.

Haskins, R. Beyond Metaphor: The Efficacy of Early Childhood Education. *American Psychogist*, Vol. 44, 1989.

Huang, G., & Howley C. Mitigating Disadvantage: Effects of Small-Scale Schooling on Student Achievement in Alaska. *Journal of Research in Rural Education*, Vol. 9, 1993.

Havighurst, Robert. Who are the Socially Disadvantaged? *Journal of Negro Education*, Vol. 40, 1965.

Hayes, Sarah H. *The Quotable Lyndon B. Johnson*. New York: Grossett & Dunlap, 1968.

Hechinger, Fred M. Public Education as the Great Equalizer. In Nelson

F. Ashline, Thomas R. Pezzullo, & Charles I. Norris, eds. *Education, Inequality, and National Policy*. Lexington, MA: Lexington Books, 1976.

Hendrie, Caroline. High Court in N.J. Ends Funding Suit. *Education Week*, May 27, 1998.

Hendrie, Caroline. N.J. Judge Urges Vast Aid Boost For Urban Schools. *Education Week*, January 28, 1998.

Herrnstein, Richard J. I.Q. *Atlantic Monthly*, September, 1971.

Herrnstein, Richard J. *I.Q. In Meritocracy*. Boston, MA: Little, Brown, 1973.

Herrnstein, Richard J., & Murray, Charles. *The Bell Curve: Intelligence and Class Structure in American Life*. New York: Free Press, 1994.

Heyns, B. Social Selection and Stratification Within Schools. *American Journal of Sociology*, Vol. 79, 1974.

Hickrod, G. Alan, McNeal, Larry, Lenz, Robert, Minorini, Paul, & Grady, Linda. Status of School Finance Constitutional Litigation. Http://www.coe.ilstu.edu/boxscore.htm.

Hinchcliffe, K. Education, Individual Earnings and Earnings Distribution. *Journal of Development Studies*, Vol. 11, 1975.

Hobbes, Thomas. *Leviathan*. Edited by W.G. Pogson Smith. London, UK: Oxford Universtiy Press, 1962.

Hoffer, Thomas B. Middle School Ability Grouping and Student Achievement in Science and Mathematics. *Educational Evaluation and Policy Analysis*, Vol. 14, 1992.

Howe, Kenneth. In Defense of Outcomes-Based Conceptions of Equal Educational Opportunity. *Educational Theory*, Vol. 39, No. 4, 1989.

Howley, C. Compounding Disadvantage: The Effects of School and District Size on Student Achievement in West Virginia. *Journal of Research in Rural Education*, Vol. 12, No. 1, 1996.

Howley, C. Synthesis of the Effects of School and District Size: What Research Says About Achievement in Small Schools and School Districts. *Journal of Rural and Small Schools*, Vol. 4, No. 1, 1989.

Hunt, John. The Psychological Basis for Using Pre-School Environment as an Antidote for Cultural Deprivation. *Merrill-Palmer Quarterly*, Vol. 10, 1964.

Hurn, Christopher J. *The Limits and Possibilities of Schooling*. 3rd edition. Boston, MA: Allyn & Bacon, 1993.

Iannaccone, Laurence. From Equity to Excellence: Political Context and Dynamics. In William Lowe Boyd & Charles Taylor Kerchner, eds. *The Politics of Excellence and Choice in Education*. New York: Falmer Press, 1987.

Jacoby, Russell, & Glauberman, Naomi. *The Bell Curve Debate: History, Documents, Opinions*. New York: Times Books, 1995.

Jencks, Christopher, et al. *Inequality*. New York: Basic Books, 1972.

Jencks, Christopher. *Who Gets Ahead? The Determinants of Economic Success in America*. New York: Basic Books, 1985.

Jencks, Christopher. *Rethinking Social Policy*. Cambridge, MA: Harvard University Press, 1992.

Jencks, Christopher, & Brown, M. The Effects of High Schools on Their Students. *Harvard Educational Review*, Vol. 45, 1975.

Jennings, John F. The Sputnik of the Eighties. *Phi Delta Kappan*, October, 1987.

Jennings, John F. *National Issues in Education: Goals 2000 and School-to-Work*. Bloomington, IN: Phi Delta Kappa Educational Foundation, 1995.

Jennings, John F. Opportunity to Learn or Opportunity to Lose? *Education Week*, November 26, 1997.

Jensen, Arthur R. How Much Can We Boost I.Q. and Scholastic Achievement? *Harvard Educational Review*, Vol. 39, 1969.

Jensen, Arthur R. *Educational Differences*. London, UK: Methuen Press, 1973.

Jensen, Arthur R. Compensatory Education and the Theory of Intelligence. *Phi Delta Kappan*, April, 1985.

Jones-Wilson, Faustine C. Equity in Education: Low Priority School Reform Movement. *Urban Review*, Vol. 18, No. 1, 1986.

Jordan, Cathie. Translating Culture: From Ethnograpchic Information to Educational Program. *Anthropology and Education Quarterly*, Vol. 16, 1985.

Kaestle, Carl F., & Smith, Marshall S. The Historical Context of the Federal Role in Education. *Harvard Educational Review*, Vol. 52, No. 4, 1982.

Kantor, Harvey, & Lowe, Robert. Class, Race, and the Emergence of Federal Education Policy. *Educational Researcher*, Vol. 24, No. 3, 1995.

Karabel, Jerome. Community Colleges and Social Stratification: Submerged Class Conflict in American Higher Education. *Harvard*

Educational Review, Vol. 42, 1972.

Kariger, R.B. The Relationship of Lane Grouping to the Socio-Economic Status of Parents of Seventh-Grade Pupils in Three Junior High Schools. *Book Abstracts*, Vol. 23, 1962.

Kateb, George. Notes On Pluralism. *Social Research*, Vol. 61, No. 3, 1994.

Kelley, Jonathan, & Klein, Herbert S. *Revolution and the Rebirth of Inequality*. Berkeley, CA: University of California Press, 1981.

Kennedy, E.M. The Head Start Transition Project: Head Start Goes to Elementary School. In E. Zigler & S.J. Styfco, eds. *Head Start and Beyond: A National Plan for Extended Childhood Intervention*. New Haven, CT: Yale University Press, 1993.

Kerckhoff, Alan. The Effects of Ability Grouping. *American Sociological Review*, Vol. 51, 1986.

Kildee, Dale E. Enacting Goals 2000: Educate America Act. In *National Issues in Education: Goals 2000 and School-to-Work*. Bloomington, IN: Phi Delta Kappa Educational Foundation, 1995.

Klein, T.W. *Program Evaluation of the Kamehameha Elementary Education Program's Reading Curriculum in Hawaii Public Schools*. Honolulu, HI: Kamehameha Schools/Bishop Estate.

Knapp, Michael S., & Woolverton, Sarah. Social Class and Schooling. In James A. Banks & Cherry A. McGee Banks, eds. *Handbook of Research on Multicultural Education*. New York: Macmillan, 1995.

Kozol, Jonathan. *Savage Inequalities*. New York: Harper Perennial, 1991.

Kozol, Jonathan. *Amazing Grace: The Lives of Children and the Conscience of a Nation*. New York: Harper Perennial, 1996.

Krouse, R., & McPherson, M. Capitalism, 'Property-Owning Democracy,' and the Welfare State. In Amy Gutman, ed. *Democracy and the Welfare State*. Princeton, NJ: Princeton University Press, 1988.

Kulick, Chen-Lin, & Kulick, James A. Effects of Ability Grouping on Secondary School Students: A Meta-Analysis of Evaluation Findings. *American Educational Research Journal*, Vol. 19, No. 3, 1982.

Kulick, Chen-Lin, & Kulick, James A. Effects of Ability Grouping on Student Achievement. *Equity and Excellence*, Vol. 23, Nos. 1-2, 1987.

Kulick, Chen-Lin, & Kulick, James A. *An Analysis of the Research on Ability Grouping*. Storrs, CT: National Research Center on the Gifted and Talented, University of Connecticut, 1992.

Kymlicka, Will. *Contemporary Political Theory*. Oxford, UK: Clarendon Press, 1990.

References

Lee, Valerie E., & Smith, Julia B. High School Size: Which Works Best and For Whom? *Educational Evaluation and Policy Analysis,* Vol. 19, No. 3, 1997.

Levin, Henry M. A Decade of Policy Developments in Improving Education and Training for Low-Income Populations. In Robert H. Haveman, ed. *A Decade of Federal Anti-Poverty Programs: Achievements, Failures, and Lessons.* New York: Academic Press, 1977.

Levine, D.U., & Havighurst, R.J. *Society and Education* (6th ed.). Boston, MA: Allyn & Bacon, 1984.

Levine, D.U., & Lezotte, L.W. *Unusually Effective Schools.* Madison, WI: The National Center for Effective Schools Research and Development, 1990.

Levine, D.U. Update on Effective Schools: Findings and Implications From Research and Practice. *Journal of Negro Education,* Vol. 59, No. 4, 1990.

Lewis, Oscar. The Culture of Poverty. *Scientific American,* Vol. 215, 1966.

Lewontin, Richard. *Not in Our Genes: Biology, Ideology, and Human Nature.* New York: Pantheon Books, 1984.

Lieberson, Stanley. *A Piece of the Pie: Blacks and White Immigrants Since 1880.* Berkely & Los Angeles, CA: University of California Press, 1980.

Lindblum, Charles E. *Politics and Markets: The World's Political-Economic Systems.* New York: Basic Books, 1977.

Locke, John. *Second Treatise of Government.* Edited by C. B. MacPherson. Indianapolis, IN: Hackett Publishing Company, 1980.

Machler, B. Grouping in the Ghetto. *Education and Urban Society,* Vol. 2, 1969.

Massell, Diane, & Fuhrman, Susan H. *Ten Years of State Education Reform, 1983-1993: Update with Four Case Studies.* New Brunswick, NJ: Rutgers University, Consortium for Policy Research in Education, 1993.

Massell, Diane, Kirst, Michael, & Hoppe, Margaret, of the Consortium for Policy Research in Education. Persistence and Change: Standards-Based Systemic Reform in Nine States. Philadelphia, PA: 1997.

Madaus, George F. A National Testing System: Manna from Above? A Historical/Technological Perspective. *Educational Assessment,* Vol. 1, 1993.

MacCallum, G.C. Negative and Positive Freedom. *Philosophical Re-*

view, Vol. 76, No. 3, 1967.

Madden, Nancy A., Slavin, Robert E., Karweit, Nancy L., Dolan, Lawrence, & Wasik, Barbara A. Success for All. *Phi Delta Kappan*, April, 1991.

Marx, Karl. *Capital* (1883). Moscow, Russia: Foreign Languages Publishing House, 1954 (Volume I) and 1959 (Volume III).

McDermott, Ray. Social Relations as Context for Learning. *Harvard Educational Review*, Vol. 47, 1977.

McDermott, Ray. Achieving School Failure: An Anthropological Approach to Illiteracy and Social Stratification. In G. Spindler, ed., *Education and Cultural Process*. Prospect Heights, IL: Waveland Press, 1987.

McDonnell, Lorraine M. Opportunity to Learn as a Research Concept and a Policy Instrument. *Educational Evaluation and Policy Analysis*, Vol. 17, No. 3, 1995.

McGiverin, Jennifer, Gilman, David, & Tillitski, Chris. A Meta-Analysis of the Relation Between Class Size and Achievement. *The Elemenatary School Journal*, Vol. 90, 1989.

McKey, R. H., Condelli, L., Ganson, H., Barrett, B., McConkey, C., & Plantz, M. *The Impact of Head Start on Children, Family, and Communities: Final Report of the Head Start Evaluation. Synthesis and Utilization Project* (DHHS Publication No. OHDS 85-31193). Washington, DC: U.S. Government Printing Office, 1985.

Mehan, Hugh. Understanding Inequality in Schools: The Contribution of Interpretive Studies. *Sociology of Education*, Vol. 65, 1992.

Meier, Deborah. Small Schools, Big Results. *The American School Board Journal*, July, 1995.

Meyer, John W. The Effects of Education as an Institution. *American Journal of Sociology*, Vol. 83, 1977.

Mill, John Stuart. *On Liberty*. New York: Bobbs-Merrill, 1956.

Miller, L. Scott. *An American Imperative: Accelerating Minority Educational Advancement*. New Haven, CT: Yale University Press, 1995.

Milner, Murray. *The Illusion of Equality*. San Francisco, CA: Jossey-Bass Inc., 1972.

Milner, Murray. Theories of Inequality. Citing not known.

Miner, Barbara. Who is Backing *The Bell Curve*? *Educational Leadership*, April, 1995.

Morgan, Harry. Assessment of Students' Behavioral Interactions During On-Task Classroom Activities. *Perceptual and Motor Skills*, Vol. 70, 1990.

Mosteller, Frederick, Light, Richard J., & Sachs, Jason A. Sustained Inquiry in Education: Lessons from Skill-Grouping and Class Size. *Harvard Educational Review*, Vol. 66, No. 4, 1996.

Murray, Charles. *Losing Ground*. New York: Basic Books, 1984.

Murray, Charles, & Richard J. Herrnstein. Race, Genes and I.Q.: An Apologia: The Case for Conservative Multiculturalism. *New Republic*, Vol. 211, No. 18, 1994.

National Commission on Excellence in Education. *A Nation at Risk: The Imperative for Educational Reform*. Printed at full length. *Elementary School Journal*, Vol. 84, No. 2, 1983.

National Council on Education Standards and Testing. *Raising Standards for American Education*. Washington, DC: National Council on Education Standards and Testing, 1992.

National Education Association (NEA). *Class Size*. Research Summary. Washington, DC: NEA Research Division, 1968.

Natriello, Gary, et al. *Schooling Disadvantaged Children: Racing Against Catastrophe*. New York: Teachers' College Press, 1990.

Nozick, Robert. *Anarchy, State, and Utopia*. New York: Basic Books, 1974.

Oakes, Jeannie. *Keeping Track: How Schools Structure Inequality*. New Haven, CT: Yale University Press, 1985.

Oakes, Jeannie, Gamoran, Adam, & Page, Reba. Curriculum Differentiation: Opportunities, Outcomes, and Meanings. *Handbook of Research on Curriculum Differentiation*, 1992.

Oakes, Jeannie, & Lipton, Martin. Detracking Schools: Early Lessons from the Field. *Phi Delta Kappan*, Vol. 73, No. 6, 1992.

Oakes, Jeannie. Can Tracking Research Inform Practice? Technical, Normative, and Political Considerations. *Educational Researcher*, Vol. 21, 1992.

Oakes, Jeannie. More Than Just Misapplied Technology: A Normative and Political Response to Hallinan on Tracking. *Sociology of Education*, Vol. 67, 1994.

Oakes, Jeannie. Opportunity-to-Learn: Can Standards-Based Reform be Equity-Based Reform?" In *75th Anniversary Commemorative Volume*. Washington, DC: National Council of Teachers of Mathematics, 1995.

O'Day, J., & Smith, M.S. Systemic Reform and Educational Opportunity. In Furhman, S. H., ed. *Designing Coherent Education Policy.* San Francisco, CA: Jossey-Bass, 1993.

Odden, A., ed. *Rethinking School Finance: An Agenda for the 1990s.* San Francisco, CA: Jossey-Bass, 1992.

Odden, A. Class Size and Student Achievement: Research-Based Policy Alternatives. *Educational Evaluation and Policy Analysis,* Vol. 12, No. 2, 1990.

Ogbu, John. Variability in Minority School Performance: A Problem in Search of an Explanation. *Anthropology and Education Quarterly,* December, 1987.

Page, Ralph. Opportunity and Its Willing Requirement. *Proceedings of the Philosophy of Education Society,* 1976.

Pallas, A.M. School Dropouts in the United States. In J.D. Stern & M.F. Williams, eds. *The Condition of Education.* Washington, DC: U.S. Government Printing Office, 1986.

Passow, A. Harry. Tackling the Reform Reports of the 1980s. *Phi Delta Kappa,.* June, 1984.

Perkinson, Henry J. *The Imperfect Panacea: American Faith in Education 1865-1965.* New York: Random House, 1968.

Persell, C.H. *Education and Inequality: The Roots and Results of Stratification in America's Schools.* New York: Free Press, 1977.

Persell, C.H. Social Class and Educational Equality. In J. Banks & C. A. McGee Banks, eds. *Multicultural Education: Issues and Perspectives.* Boston, MA: Allyn & Bacon, 1993.

Peterson, Paul E. Did the Commissions Say Anything? *Education and Urban Society,* Vol. 17, No. 2, 1985.

Pincus, Fred L. From Equity to Excellence: The Rebirth of Educational Conservatism. *Social Policy,* Winter, 1984.

Plato. *The Republic.* Translated by Francis MacDonald Cornford. London, UK: Oxford University Press, 1941.

Plecki, Margaret. The Relationship Between Elementary School Size and Student Achievement. A paper presented at the annual meeting of the American Educational Research Association, April 3-7, 1991.

Plomin, Robert. Environment and Genes: Determinants of Behavior. *American Psychologist,* February, 1989.

Podeschi, Ronald, & Hackbarth, David. The Cries for Excellence: Echoes from the Past. *Educational Forum,* Vol. 50, No. 4, 1986.

Porter, Andrew. The Uses and Misuses of Opportunity-to-Learn Standards. *Educational Researcher*, January-February, 1995.

Portes, Alejandro, & Wilson, Kenneth L. Black-White Differences in Educational Attainment. *American Sociological Review*, Vol. 43, No. 3, 1976.

Psacharopoulos, George. *Earnings and Education in OECD Countries*. Paris, France: OECD, 1975.

Psacharopoulos, George, & Tilak, Jandhyala. Education and Wage Earnings. In Marvin C. Alkin, ed. *Encyclopedia of Educational Research*. New York: Macmillan, 1992.

Puma, M.J., Jones, C.C., Rock, D., & Fernandez, R. *Prospects: The Congressionally Mandated Study of Educational Growth and Opportunity*. Interim Report. Bethesda, MD: Abt Associates, 1993.

Rawls, John. *A Theory of Justice*. Cambridge, MA: Harvard University Press, 1971.

Reissman, Frank. *The Culturally Deprived Child*. New York: Harper & Row, 1962.

Richardson, Virginia et al. *School Children at Risk*. London, UK: Falmer Press, 1989.

Rist, Ray. On Understanding the Processes of Schooling: The Contributions of Labelling Theory. In J. Karabel & A.H. Halsey, eds. *Power and Ideology in Education*. New York: Oxford Press, 1977.

Robinson, Glenn E., & Wittebols, J.H. *Class Size Research: A Related Cluster Analysis for Decision Making*. Arlington, VA: Educational Research Service, 1986.

Rosenbaum, James E. *Making Inequality: The Hidden Curriculum of High School Tracking*. New York: John Wiley & Sons, 1976.

Rosenthal, Robert, & Jacobson, Lenore. *Pygmalion in the Classroom*. New York: Holt, Rinehart, & Winston, 1968.

Ross, Steven M., Smith, Lana J., Slavin, Robert E., & Madden, Nancy A. Improving the Academic Success of Disadvantaged Children: An Examination of Success For All. *Psychology in the Schools*, Vol. 34, No. 2, 1997.

Ross, Steven M, Smith, L. J., & Casey, J. *1994-1995 Fort Wayne, Indiana Success For All Results*. Memphis, TN: Center for Research on Educational Policy, The University of Memphis, 1995.

Rothman R. "Delivery Standards" for Schools at Heart of New Policy Debate. *Education Week*, April, 7, 1993.

Rousseau, Jean-Jacques. *On Social Contract*. Translated by Julia

Conaway Bondanella. New York: W.W. Norton & Company, 1988.

Salganik, L., & Celebuski, C. *Educational Attainment Study: Preliminary Tables*. Washington, DC: Pelavin Associates, 1987.

Sandel, Michael. *Liberalism and the Limits of Justice*. Cambridge, UK: Cambridge University Press, 1982.

Sandel, Michael. Morality and the Liberal Ideal. *The New Republic*, May, 7, 1984.

Schaar, John. Equality of Opportunity and Beyond. In J.R. Pennock & J.W. Chapman, eds, *Nomos IX: Equality*. New York: Atherton Press, 1967.

Schaar, John. Equality of Opportunity and the Just Society. In Blocker & Smith, eds., *John Rawls' Theory of Social Justice: An Introduction*. Athens: OH: Ohio University Press, 1980.

Schaefer, Thomas E. One More Time: How Do You Get Both Equality and Excellence in Education? *The Journal of Educational Thought*, Vol. 24, No. 1, 1990.

Scheffler, Samuel. Responsibility, Reactive Attitudes, and Liberalism in Philosophy and Politics. *Philosophy and Public Affairs*, Vol. 21, No. 4, 1992.

Schweinhart, L.J., Barnes, H.V., & Weikart, D.P. *Significant Benefits: The High/Scope Perry Preschool Study Through Age 27*. (Monographs of the High/Scope Educational Research Foundation, No. 10). Ypsilanti, MI: High/Scope Press, 1993.

Sebring, P., Campbell, B. Glusberg, M., Spencer, B., Singleton, M., & Turner, M. *High School and Beyond: 1980 Sophomore Cohort Third Follow-Up (1986). Data File User's Manual*. Chicago, IL: National Opinion Research Center, University of Chicago, 1987.

Sen, Amartya. *Inequality Reexamined*. Cambridge, MA: Harvard University Press, 1992.

Sewell, William H., & Hauser, Robert M. Causes and Consequences of Higher Education: Modes of the Status Attainment Process. In Sewell, Hauser, & Feathermen, eds. *Schooling and Achievement in American Society*. New York: Academic Press, 1976.

Sherman, J.D. *Dropping Out of School: Causes and Consequences for Male and Female Youth*. Washington, DC: Pelavin Associates, 1987.

Singer, Alan. Multiculturalism and Democracy. The Promise of Multicultural Education. *Social Education*, Vol. 56, No. 2, 1992.

Sizer, Theodore R. *Horace's Compromise: The Dilemma of the American High School*. Boston, MA: Houghton Mifflin, 1984.

References

Skerry, Peter. The Charmed Life of Head Start. *Public Interest*, Fall, 1983.

Slavin, Robert E. Ability Grouping and Student Achievement in Elementary Schools: A Best Evidence Synthesis. *Review of Educational Research*, Vol. 57, No. 3, 1987.

Slavin, Robert E. Achievement Effects of Ability Grouping in Secondary Schools: A Best Evidence Synthesis. *Review of Educational Research*, Vol. 60, No. 3, 1990.

Slavin, Robert E., & Jomills H. Braddock II. Ability Grouping: On the Wrong Track. *College Board Review*, Vol. 168, 1993.

Slavin, Robert E. Synthesis of Research on Cooperative Learning. *Educational Leadership*, Vol. 48, 1991.

Slavin, Robert E. Chapter 1: A Vision for the Next Quarter Century. *Phi Delta Kappan*, April, 1991.

Slavin, Robert E., Madden, N. A., Dolan, L. J., Wasik, B. A., Ross, S. M., Smith, L. J., & Dianda, M. Success For All: A Summary of Research. *Journal of Education for Students Placed At Risk*, Vol. 1, No. 1, 1996.

Smith, David G. Liberalism. In *International Encyclopedia of the Social Sciences*. New York: The Free Press, 1968.

Smith, Marshall S., & Scoll, Brett W. The Clinton Human Capital Agenda. *Teachers College Record*, Vol. 96, No. 3, 1995.

Snyderman, Mark, & Rothman, Stanley. Survey of Expert Opinion on Intelligence and Aptitude Testing. *American Psychologist*, February, 1987.

Sorenson, Aagee B., & Hallinan, Maureen T. Race Effects on the Assignment to Ability Groups. In Peterson, Penelope L., Wilkerson, L. C., & Hallinan, Maureen T., eds. *The Social Context of Instruction*. Orlando, FL: Academic Press, 1984.

Sowell, Thomas. New Light on the Black I.Q. Controversy. *New York Times Magazine*, March 27, 1977.

Spindler, G., & Spindler, L. The Processes of Culture and Person: Cultural Therapy and Culturally Diverse Schools. In P. Phelan & A.L. Davidson, eds. *Renegotiating Cultural Diversity in American Schools*. New York: Teachers College Press, 1993.

Stedman, J.B., Salganik, L.H., & Celebuski, C.A. *Dropping Out: The Educational Vulnerability of At-Risk Youth*. Washington, DC: Congressional Research Service, 1988.

Stedman, Lawrence C., & Smith, Marshall S. Recent Reform Proposals for American Education. *Contemporary Education Review*, Vol. 2,

No. 2, 1983.

Stickney, Benjamin D., & Marcus, Laurence R. Education and the Disadvantaged 20 Years Later. *Phi Delta Kappan*, April, 1985.

Strawson, P.F. Freedom and Resentment. In Gary Watson, ed. *Free Will*. Oxford, UK: Oxford University Press, 1982.

Strickland, Charles E. Sputnik Reform Revisited. *Educational Studies*, Vol. 16, No. 1, 1985.

Strike, Kenneth. The Ethics of Resource Allocation in Education. In D.H. Monk & Julie Underwood, eds. *Micro-Level School Finance: Issues and Implications*. Cambridge, MA: Ballanger, 1988.

Strike, Kenneth. The Moral Role of Schooling in a Liberal Democratic Society. In Gerald Grant, ed. *Review of Educational Research*. Washington, DC: American Educational Research Association, 1991.

Strike, Kenneth. *Educational Policy and the Just Society*. Urbana, IL: University of Illinois Press, 1982.

Strike, Kenneth. *Liberal Justice and the Marxist Critique of Education*. New York: Routledge Press, 1989.

Stringfield, S., & Yoder, N. Toward a Model of Elementary Grades Chapter 1 Effectiveness. In H.C. Waxman, J.W. de Felix, J.E. Anderson, & H.P. Baptiste, Jr., eds. *Students At Risk in At-Risk Schools*. Newbury Park, CA: Corwin Press, 1992.

Summers, A.A., & Wolfe, B.L. *Equality of Educational Opportunity Quantified: A Production-Function Approach*. Philadelphia, PA: Department of Research, Federal Reserve Bank of Philadelphia, 1975.

Sykes, Gary, & Plastrik, Peter. *Standard-Setting as Educational Reform*. Washington, DC: ERIC Clearinghouse on Teacher Education, American Association of Colleges for Teacher Education, 1993.

Takanishi, Ruby, & DeLeon, Patrick H. A Head Start For the 21st Century. *American Psychologist*, February, 1994.

Task Force on Education for Economic Growth. *Action for Excellence: A Comprehensive Plan to Improve Our Nation's Schools*. Denver, CO: Education Commission of the States, 1983.

Tawney, R.H. *Equality*. New York: Harcourt, Brace, 1931.

Taylor, Charles. Political Theory and Political Practice. In *Social Theory and Political Practice*. Oxford, UK: Clarendon Press, 1983.

Taylor, Charles. Atomism. In Alkis Kontos, ed. *Powers, Possessions and Freedoms: Essays in Honor of C.B. Macpherson*. Toronto, Ontario, Canada: University of Toronto Press, 1979.

Taylor, W., & Piche, D. *A Report on Shortchanging Children: The Impact of Fiscal Inequity on the Education of Students at Risk.* Washington, DC: Government Printing Office, 1990.

Tesconi, Charles A., & Hurwitz, Emanuel, Jr. *Education for Whom?* New York: Dodd, Mead, & Company, 1974.

Tharp. Roland G. The Effective Instruction of Comprehension. *Reading Research Quarterly,* Vol. 17, No. 4, 1982.

Tharp. Roland G. Psychocultural Variables and Constants: Effects on Teaching and Learning in Schools. *American Psychologist,* February, 1989.

Tharp. Roland G. *Rousing Minds to Life: Teaching, Learning, and Schooling in Social Context.* Cambridge, UK: Cambridge University Press, 1988.

Tozer, Steven E., Violas, Paul C., & Senese, Guy. *School and Society: Historical and Contemporary Perspectives.* Boston, MA: McGraw-Hill, 1998.

Twentieth Century Fund Task Force on Federal Elementary and Secondary Education Policy. *Making the Grade.* New York: Twentieth Century Fund, 1983.

Tyler, Ralph W. The Federal Role in Education. *Public Interest,* Vol. 34, 1974.

U.S. Bureau of the Census. *The Hispanic Population in the United States: March 1988 (Advance Report).* (Current Population Reports, Series P-20, No. 431). Washington, DC: U.S. Government Printing Office, 1988.

U.S. Bureau of the Census. *Money Income and Poverty Status in the United States: 1987 (Advance Data from the March 1988 Current Population Survey).* (Current Population Reports, Series P-60, No. 161). Washington, DC: U.S. Government Printing Office, 1988.

U.S. Bureau of the Census. *Household and Family Characteristics: March 1987.* (Current Population Reports, Series P-20, No. 424). Washington, DC: U.S. Government Printing Office, 1988.

U.S. Bureau of the Census. *Marital Status and Living Arrangements: March 1988.* (Current Population Reports, Series P-20, No. 433). Washington, DC: U.S. Government Printing Office, 1989.

U.S. Government Printing Office. *Goals 2000: Educate America Act of 1994.* Pub. L. No. 103-227. 103rd Congress, 2nd Session. Washington, DC: U.S. Government Printing Office.

Valentine, C.A. *Culture and Poverty*. Chicago, IL: University of Chicago Press, 1968.

Valentine, C.A. Deficit, Difference, ad Bicultural Models of Afro-American Behavior. *Harvard Educational Review*, Vol. 41, No. 2, 1971.

Walker, Reagan. Entire Kentucky School System is Ruled Invalid. *Education Week*, June 14, 1989.

Walzer, Michael. In Defense of Equality. *Dissent*, Fall, 1973.

Wells, A.S, & Oakes, Jeannie. Potential Pitfals of Systemic Reform. Early Lessons From Research on Detracking. *Sociology of Education*, Extra issue, 1996.

Wheelock, Anne. From Tracking to High Quality Heterogeneous Instruction. In Ann Turnbaugh Lockwood, ed. *Tracking: Conflicts and Resolutions*. Thousand Oakes, CA: Corwin Press, 1996.

Wheelock, Anne. *Crossing the Tracks: How "Untracking" Can Save America's Schools*. New York: W.W. Norton, 1992.

Williams, Bernard. The Idea of Equality. In Laslett & Runciman, eds. *Philosophy, Politics, and Society*. Oxford, UK: Blackwell, 1962.

Wilson, William J. *The Truly Disadvantaged: The Inner City, the Underclass, and Public Policy*. Chicago, IL: University of Chicago Press, 1987.

Woodhead, M. When Psychology Informs Public Policy: The Case of Early Childhood Intervention. *American Psychologist*, Vol. 43, 1988.

Word, E., Johnston, J., Bain, H.P., Fulton, B.D., Zaharias, J.B., Lintz, M.N., Achilles, C.M., Folger, J., & Breda, C. *Student/Teacher Achievement Ratio (STAR), Tennessee's Class Size Study: Final Summary Report, 1985-1990*. Nashville, TN: Tennessee State Department of Education, 1990.

Word, E., Johnston, J., Bain, H.P., Fulton, B.D., Zaharias, J.B., Lintz, M.N., Achilles, C.M., Folger, J., & Breda, C. *The State of Tennessee's Student/Teacher Achievement Ratio (STAR) Project: Technical Report 1985-1990*. Nashville, TN: Tennessee State Department of Education, 1994.

Young, Michael. *The Rise of the Meritocracy*. London, UK: Thames & Hudson, 1958.

Zigler, Edward, & Berman, Winnie. Discerning the Future of Early Childhood Intervention. *American Psychologist*, August, 1983.

Zigler, Edward, & Berman, Winnie. Head Start: Criticisms in a Constructive Context. *American Psychologist*, February, 1994.

Index
of Authors

About
the Author

Gregory J. Fritzberg received a Bachelor's of Arts degree from Pacific Lutheran University in 1985, a Master's of Arts degree from Fuller Theological Seminary in 1992, and the degree of Doctor of Philosophy in Educational Foundations from the University of Washington in 1998. Formerly a teacher at a public alternative high school in South Seattle, Dr. Fritzberg has held an Assistant Professorship in Education at Whitworth College in Spokane, Washington, since 1997. He lives in Spokane with his wife Marie, daughter Emma Jane, and son Ethan James.